Harriet Elizabeth Prescott Spofford

New-England legends

Harriet Elizabeth Prescott Spofford

New-England legends

ISBN/EAN: 9783337150822

Printed in Europe, USA, Canada, Australia, Japan

Cover: Foto ©ninafisch / pixelio.de

More available books at **www.hansebooks.com**

New-England Legends.

BY

HARRIET PRESCOTT SPOFFORD.

WITH ILLUSTRATIONS.

BOSTON:

JAMES R. OSGOOD AND COMPANY,

(Late Ticknor & Fields, and Fields, Osgood, & Co.)

1871.

HAND, AVERY, & FRYE, PRINTERS, 3 CORNHILL, BOSTON.

THE following hastily-prepared sketches, originally published in less permanent form, are collected at the request of indulgent readers, and offered with all due apology for their incompleteness. H. P. S.

NEWBURYPORT, MASS., Aug. 1, 1871.

CONTENTS.

The True Account of Captain Kidd . . .

Charlestown . . . .

Salem . . . .

Newburyport . . . .

Dover . . . .

Portsmouth . . . .

ILLUSTRATIONS.

	PAGE.
KIDD KILLS WILLIAM MOORE	3
ESCAPE OF THE MYSTERIOUS LADY FROM THE URSULINE CONVENT ON MT. BENEDICT	11
RUINS OF THE URSULINE CONVENT	13
REV. GEORGE BURROUGHS ACCUSED OF WITCHCRAFT	17
CAPT. BOARDMAN ORDERS THE BRITISH FLAG TO BE STRUCK	25
GRAND-DAUGHTER OF MAJOR WALDRON ALONE IN THE WOODS	33
FRANCES DEERING MAKING SIGNAL	37

THE TRUE ACCOUNT OF CAPTAIN KIDD.

The islands about the harbors of all our New England rivers are so wild, and would seem to have offered so many advantages, that they have always been supposed, by the ruder population, to be the hiding-place of piratical treasures, and particularly of Captain Kidd's ; and the secretion, among rocks and sands, of chests of jewels stripped from noble Spanish ladies who have walked the awful plank, with shot-bags full of diamonds, and ingots of pure gold, is one of the tenets of the vulgar faith. This belief has ranged up and down the whole shore with more freedom than the pirates ever did, and the legends on the subject are legion —from the old Frenchman of Passamaquoddy Bay to the wild stories of the Jersey and Carolina sandbars too countless for memory, the Fireship off Newport, the Shrieking Woman of Marblehead, and the Lynn Mariner who, while burying his treasure in a cave, was sealed up alive by a thunderbolt that cleft the rock, and whom some one, under spiritual inspiration, spent lately a dozen years in vain endeavor to unearth. The parties that have equipped themselves with hazel-rods and spades, and proceeded, at the dead of night, in search of these riches, without turning their heads or uttering the Divine Name, and, digging till they struck metal, have met with all manner of ghostly appearances, from the little naked negro sitting and crying on the edge of the hogshead of doubloons, to the ball of fire sailing straight up the creek, till it hangs trembling on the tide just opposite the excavation into which it shoots with the speed of lightning, so terrifying and bewildering the treasure-seekers that when all is over they fail to find again the place of their late labor—the parties that have met with these adventures would, perhaps, cease to waste much more of their time in such pursuits in this part of the country if they knew that Captain Kidd had never landed north of Block Island until, with fatal temerity, he brought his vessel into Boston, and that every penny of his gains was known and was accounted for, while as to Bradish, Tew, and the rest of that gentry, they wasted everything as they went in riotous living, and could never have had a dollar to hide, and no disposition to hide it if they had ; and whatever they did possess they took with them when, quietly abandoning their ships to the officers of the law, they went up the creeks and rivers in boats, and dispersed themselves throughout the country.

Ever since the time of Jason there have been sea-robbers, and at one period they so infested the Mediterranean—owning a thousand galleys and four hundred cities, it is said—that Pompey was sent out with a fleet and a force of soldiery to extirpate them. In later times there were tribes of lawless men associated together in hunting the cattle of the West Indian islands, curing the flesh, and exchanging it in adjacent settlements ; they held all property in common, and were called Buccaneers, from the word "boucan," a Carib term for preserved meat. By the mistaken policy of the viceroys of the islands, who, in order to reduce them to less lawless lives, exterminated all the cattle, these men were driven to the sea, and became in time the celebrated freebooters, or "Brethren of the Coast." The bull of Pope Alexander VI., by authority of which Spain and Portugal claimed all American discoveries, caused England, France and the Netherlands to combine in the Western Hemisphere, whatever quarrels came to hand in the Eastern, and to ravage the common enemy—so that letters-of-marque were constantly issued by them to all adventurers, without requiring any condemnation of prizes or account of proceedings, by which means these countries virtually created a system of piracy, and Sir Francis Drake's sack of St. Domingo, and the subsequent pillage of Pernambuco, were in nowise different from the exploits of the brutal Olonois, Van Horn, and Brodely, upon the opulent Spanish cities of the Main. As the trade with the East and West Indies increased, these freebooters ceased to sail under any color but their own, the black flag ; no longer left their ships to march through tropical swamps and forests, to float on rafts down rivers of a hundred cataracts, to scale mountains, and fall, as if out of the clouds, on the devoted cities of the Isthmus of Darien, the silver and gold of whose cathedrals, palaces and treasure-houses were worth the labor ; nor did they confine themselves on sea to overhauling the Spanish galleon sitting deep in the water with her lading from the Mexican and Peruvian mines ; but they made their attacks on the great slow ship of the Asiatic waters, and when their suppression became vital to commerce, and all powers united against them, they possessed themselves of sumptuous retreats in Madagascar and the Indian Ocean, where they had their seraglios, and lived in fabulous splendor and luxury. As this race, hunted on sea and enervated on land, died out, their place was taken by others, and expeditions came gradually to be fitted out from the colonies of New England, while Virginia, the Carolinas, and even the Quakers of Philadelphia, afforded them a market for their robberies. When these also in their time abandoned their profession, they made their homes, some in the Carolinas, some in Rhode Island, and some on the south shore of Long Island, where their descendants are among the most respectable of the community.

To none of these did Captain Kidd belong; and, previous to the last two years of his life, he was esteemed a good citizen, and as honest a sea-captain as ever sailed out of New York, to which place he belonged, and where, in the Surrogate's office, is still preserved his marriage certificate, that classifies him as Gentleman. During the war with France he had been master of a ship in the neighborhood of the Caribbean Sea, and had valiantly come to the assistance of a British man-of-war, and the two together had vanquished a fleet of six French frigates; it was testified upon his trial that he had been a mighty man in the West Indies, and that he had refused to go a pirateering, upon which his men had seized his ship; and it was on account of his public services there that the General Assembly of New York had paid him a bounty of one hundred and fifty pounds—a great sum in those days; and the probability is, that, being made a bone of contention between political parties, exactly what he was applauded for doing at one time he was hung for doing at another.

The American seas being greatly troubled by pirates, early in 1695 the King summoned the Earl of Bellomont before him, and told him that, having come to the determination to put an end to the increasing piratical tendencies of his colonies, he had chosen him as the most suitable person to be invested with the government of New York and New England. The earl at once set about devising the readiest means for the execution of the King's purpose, and Robert Livingston, chancing then to be in London, and being acquainted with the earl, introduced to him William Kidd, who, having left his wife and children in New York, was also then in London, as a person who had secured some fame in engagements with the French, a man of honor and intrepidity, and one who, knowing the haunts of the pirates, was very fit to command the expedition against them which Bellomont and others were planning. Livingston became Kidd's surety, a kindness that the latter always remembered, as he threatened, on his return two years afterward, to sell his sloop, and indemnify Livingston out of the proceeds, if Bellomont did not surrender the bond.

It was at first proposed that Kidd should have a British frigate, but hardly daring to give him that—which hesitation in itself indicates how far the great lords were really implicated in his transactions—a ship was purchased for six thousand pounds, Kidd and Livingston being at one-fifth of the expense, and the rest being borne by the Earls of Bellomont and Romney, the Lord Chancellor Somers, the Lord

High Admiral, the Duke of Shrewsbury, and Sir Edward Harrison, and they agreed to give the King, who entered into it very heartily, a tenth of the profits of the affair. Kidd was somewhat averse to the plan, and seriously demurred, it is believed, but was threatened by the men of power that his own ship should be detained and taken from him if he persisted, and accordingly he yielded, and in 1696 was regularly commissioned under two separate parchments, one to cruise against the French, and the other—an extraordinary one, but issued under the Great Seal, empowering him to proceed against the pirates of the American seas, and really given for the purpose of authorizing him to dispose of such property as he might capture. He had orders to render his accounts to the Earl of Bellomont, remotely and securely in New England; and the Adventure Galley, a private armed ship of thirty guns and eighty men, was brought to the buoy in the Nore at the latter end of February, and on the 23d of April, 1696, he sailed in her from Plymouth, reaching New York in July, and bringing in a French ship, valued at three hundred and fifty pounds, which he had taken on the passage, and which he there condemned.

In New York he invited men to enter his service, by notices posted in the streets and presenting large offers of booty after forty shares for himself and the ship should be deducted; and increasing his crew to more than one hundred and fifty men, he went to Madeira, then to several of the West Indian ports, and afterward to Madagascar, the coast of Malabar, and to Bab's Key, an island at the entrance of the Red Sea, where he lay in wait for the Mocha fleet, then preparing to sail. It is evident that he went outside of his nominal instructions by thus leaving the American for the Asiatic waters; but it is also evident that he understood he was to be supported by the people of power who were behind him at home, and believed himself to be only following out their intentions; and the man who had been encouraged to rob one ship had not, perhaps, sufficient refinement of discrimination to think any different matter of robbing another. Moreover, having come across and captured no vessel since leaving New York, he might naturally have felt that his owners were expecting more of him, and thus have resolved on something desperate. At any rate he did not consider himself to be going outside of his duty, or to be appearing in any questionable light, when, on his voyage out, he met the ship carrying the ambassador to the Great Mogul, and exchanged courtesies therewith.

Tired out with his want of success, when anchored at Bab's Key, he sent boats to bring the first news of the sailing of the Mocha fleet, established a lookout on the hills of the island, and told his men that now he would freight the Adventure Galley with gold and silver when the fleet came out, though it was found that many of its ships belonged to friendly nations, and it was convoyed by an English and a Dutch man-of-war. Kidd, however, sailed into the midst of the fleet, which fired at him first, and returning the fire with one or two ineffectual shots, he hauled off and left it to pursue its course. Sailing then for the coast of Malabar, a couple of months afterward Kidd took a Moorish vessel belonging to Aden, but commanded by an Englishman, and finding but little of

"KIDD SNATCHED UP AN IRON-BOUND BUCKET AND STRUCK WILLIAM MOORE A BLOW ON THE HEAD, OF WHICH HE DIED NEXT DAY."

value in the prize, he had her men hoisted by the arms and beaten with the flat of a cutlass to make them reveal what they had done with their money—a punishment which, whether severe or not for that semi-barbarous era, was, with two exceptions, the only act of personal cruelty of which he was ever accused; and people whom, if the general idea of him were true, he would have dispatched with a bullet, he simply kept in the hold till, inquiry for them being over, he dismissed them. He obtained from this vessel some coffee, pepper, and Arabian gold, and some myrrh, with which the extravagant rogue pitched his ship. Going further out to sea again, he next encountered a Portuguese man-of-war, but after a brief engagement withdrew with ten men wounded, and returned presently to the coast of Malabar. Here, his cooper having been killed by the natives, he "served them in pretty much the same way," says one writer, "as the officers of our late South Sea Exploring Expedition served the Fijians, burning their houses and shooting one of the murderers." This, however, was one of the other instances of cruelty to which reference has just been made, the murderer being bound to a tree and shot at in turn by all the retaliators. Shortly after this, Captain Kidd fell in with the ship Royal Captain, which he visited, and whose officers he entertained on board the Adventure Galley; but some of her crew having told that there were Greeks and others on board with much wealth of precious stones, the piratical spirit of his men led to mutinous desires and expressions; and, in a rage with those who had wished to board and rob the Royal Captain, Kidd snatched up an iron-bound bucket, and struck William Moore, the gunner and chief grumbler, a blow on the head, of which he died next day. Kidd remarked to his surgeon that the death of the gunner did not trouble him so much as other passages of his voyage, as he had friends in England who could easily bring him off for that; and he himself had it urged as a virtuous act rather than otherwise, since done to prevent both piracy and mutiny.

Still on the coast of Malabar, in November he ran across another Moorish vessel, and artfully hoisted the French colors, upon which the Moor did the same. "By —— I have I catched you!" he cried; "you are a free prize to England!" and making easy conquest of her, he caused one Le Roy, a French passenger, to act the part of master, and to show a pretended French pass, upon which he declared her formally a prize to England, as if observing again the prescribed forms, and intending to claim for his conduct, should he ever need to do so, the protection of the commission authorizing him to take French ships. In the course of the next month, December, he captured a Moorish ketch of fifty tons, and turned her adrift; took about four hundred pounds' worth from a Portuguese, and sunk her near Calcutta; and then made prize of an Armenian vessel of four hundred tons, called the Quedagh Merchant, and sometimes the Scuddee, and commanded by an English man—the entire value of the latter capture being sixty-four thousand pounds, of which Kidd's share was about sixteen thousand. Kidd then went to Madagascar, where, having exchanged all the equipments of the Adventure Galley for dust and bar gold and silver, silks, gold-cloth, precious stones, and spices, he burned that ship, which was leaking badly, and took to the Quedagh Merchant, refusing a ransom of thirty thousand rupees which the Armenians came, crying and wringing their hands, to offer him.

Here, too, he is said to have met with one of the East India Company's ships, Captain Culliford, turned pirate. It was clearly his duty, under his commission, to offer battle at once; but, instead of anything of the kind, it was testified on the trial that when the pirates, with bated breath, sent out a boat to inquire concerning his intentions, he drank with them, in a kind of lemonade called "bomboo," damnation to his own soul if he ever harmed them, and exchanged gifts with Culliford, receiving some silk and four hundred pounds in return for some heavy ordnance. Kidd denied that he had ever been aboard of Culliford, and declared that, when he proposed to attack him, his men said they would rather fire two shots into him than one into Culliford; that they stole his journal, broke open his chest and rifled it, plundered his ammunition, and threatened his life so that he was obliged to barricade himself in his cabin—his statement being borne out in some degree by the fact that here ninety-five of his men deserted to Captain Culliford, as if their own master were not sufficiently piratical, whereupon, recruiting a handful of men, he sailed immediately for the West Indies. He declared further that he did not go on board the Quedagh Merchant until after the desertion of these men, which left only about a dozen in his crew—not enough to keep his leaking craft from sinking.

But the capture of the Quedagh Merchant had been reported home by the East India Company, and directions had been issued to all the American governors and viceroys to seize him wherever he should appear. At Anguilla he learned that he had been officially proclaimed a pirate, and failing to obtain any provisions either there or at St. Thomas, at which latter place he was not even allowed to land, he went to Curaçoa, from whence intelligence of his whereabouts was forwarded to England, and the man-of-war Queensborough was sent in pursuit of him.

Kidd was aware that he had been upon a hazardous enterprise, so far as the risks at home were considered, to say nothing of the risks at sea; and whether he was conscious that he had exceeded his instructions, too eagerly misinterpreting them, or whether he knew that it is a way with the great to sacrifice those who compromise them too seriously, he prepared himself for any fortune: he determined to go to New York, and prove for himself what protection and countenance he now had to expect from Bellomont and the others; but he also determined to venture as little as possible, and he accordingly bought the sloop Antonia—though excusing this afterward to the earl by saying that his men, frightened by the proclamation, had wished to run the ship ashore, and so many of them left him that again he had not enough to handle the ropes, which must have been untrue—loaded her with his silks, muslins, jewels, bullion and gold-dust (the rest of his booty, consisting of bales of coarse goods, sugar, iron, rice, wax, opium, saltpetre and anchors, he left in the Quedagh Merchant, moored on the south side of Hispaniola, with twenty guns in the hold and thirty mounted, and twenty men, with his mate in command)—and sailed in her for New York; intimating, by his action, a doubt of his reception, though that might well be accounted for by a knowledge of the King's proclamation, but just as plainly intimating that he had reason to rely on the promises of Bellomont and the rest of that royal stock company in piracy:

Meanwhile Bellomont had been delayed from entering upon his official life by one thing and another, until two years had elapsed from the time of Kidd's departure from England. On arriving in New York, he heard of the rumored career which Kidd was running, and presently the news having reached England, and an account of the public sentiment about it there being returned to him, Bellomont felt that very active measures were necessary in order to exculpate himself, the Ministry and the King from the popular accusation of participating in Kidd's robberies, and took every step necessary for his apprehension.

Needing some repairs before reaching his destination, Kidd very cautiously put into Delaware Bay, where he landed a chest belonging to one Gillam, an indubitable pirate, who had been a Mohammedan, and who now returned, a passenger from Madagascar. The news spreading up the coast, an armed sloop went after Kidd, but failed to find him, and he reached the eastern end of Long Island without being overhauled. Entering the Sound, he dispatched a letter to Bellomont, and from Oyster Bay sent loving greeting to his family.

and a lawyer, by the name of Emot, came down from New York and went on board the Antonia. Learning that the Earl of Bellomont was in Boston, Kidd altered his course for Rhode Island, and, arriving there, sent Mr. Emot to Boston to secure a promise of safety from Bellomont if he should land; a promise granted on condition of its proving that Emot told the truth—he having asserted that Kidd's men locked him up while they committed piracies. Kidd then went to Block Island, and wrote to Bellomont again, protesting his innocence, urging the care he had taken of the owner's interests, and sending Lady Bellomont a present of jewels of the value of sixty pounds, which Bellomont had her keep lest she should offend the giver and prevent the developments that he desired, though afterward surrendering and adding them to the general inventory of Kidd's effects. While at Block Island he was joined by his wife and children, under the care of a Mr. Clark; he then gratefully went out of his way in order to land Mr. Clark on Gardiner's Island, as that gentleman wished to return to New York; and although Kidd himself did not go ashore at the latter place, he left with Mr. Gardiner a portion of his treasure afterward abandoned to the Commissioners sent for it by the Governor. While lying here, three sloops from New York came down and were loaded with goods, which were, however, all recovered—Kidd maintaining, with so much paucity of invention as to resemble the truth, that it was his men and not he who shipped them off. Meanwhile the earl sent down Duncan Campbell, the postmaster at Boston, to invite Captain Kidd to that port, telling him that if innocent he might safely come in, and he would intercede for his pardon; and Kidd straightway headed the Antonia for Boston, reaching there on the 1st of July and appearing publicly upon the streets. Hearing of his arrival, the earl sent for him, and, refusing to see him without witnesses, examined him before the Council, directed him to draw up a narrative of his proceedings, and dismissed him. Bellomont, however, kept a watch upon his movements, as he both desired and needed his arrest, but thought it expedient to use friendly means in order to discover the extent of his outrages and the disposition of the property acquired through them. At the end of the week, Kidd showing no intention to unbosom himself in that wise, and it being feared that he meant to make off, he was arrested and committed to prison, though not till he had made a valiant opposition and had drawn his sword upon the King's officers—the arrest taking place near the door of the earl's lodgings, into which Kidd rushed and ran toward him, followed by the constables. His sloop, on that, was immediately appraised, its contents taken possession of by certain Commissioners appointed for that purpose, his papers, containing accounts of his buried treasure and of that in Mr. Gardiner's hands, were opened, and all the property was finally delivered to the earl, with an inventory of one thousand one hundred and eleven ounces of gold, two thousand three hundred and fifty-three ounces of silver, three-score jewels, and bags, bales and pieces of goods about as valuable as the precious metals. Mrs. Kidd's property, which included several pieces of plate, nearly three hundred dollars of her own and twenty-five crowns of her maid's, was taken out of her temporary lodgings in the house of Duncan Campbell, at the time when search was made for a bag of gold-dust and ingots of the value of a thousand pounds, that Kidd had intended for a gift to Lady Bellomont, and that was found between two sea-beds; but on petition the Governor and Council restored to Mrs. Kidd her own. His wife—to whom he had been but a few years married—accompanying him with her children, her maid and all that she possessed, shows that Kidd had no intention of being surprised and overmastered; but on the contrary, if worse came to worst, that he had meant to take her back to the Quedagh Merchant and find a home in some place beyond the pale of British justice; while retaining her affection, and caring to retain it, is in itself a sort of testimony that he was hardly so black as he has been painted. Ten days after his arrest news came that the mate of the Quedagh Merchant, left in command, had taken out her cargo, removed it to Curaçoa, and had then set her on fire, and the mariner who brought the intelligence had seen her burning. That was a dark day, doubtless, to Captain Kidd, but not so dark as others yet to come.

A ship-of-war had now been dispatched from England to take Captain Kidd over there, but being delayed by inclement weather, and putting back in a storm after he was on board, by the time it arrived in the Thames all England was in a state of excitement over his alleged partnership with several of the Ministers, and their apparent determination not to bring him to justice; and from a common malefactor he became the lofty subject of a state trial.

On his arrival the House of Commons addressed the King, asking to have Kidd's trial postponed until the next Parliament, that there might be time for the transmission of all the existing documents having any relation to his affairs; and he was accordingly confined in Newgate until the next year, when the papers were laid before the House, together with a petition from Cogi Baba, on behalf of himself and other Armenians, subjects of the King of Persia, setting forth all the facts of the Quedagh Merchant's capture, and praying for Kidd's examination and their own relief. Cogi Baba was ordered before the House, and Kidd himself was produced at the bar, and afterward remanded to prison. A motion was then made in the House to declare void the grant made to the Earl of Bellomont and others of all the treasure taken by Kidd, but it was negatived, and the House of Commons then requested the King to have Kidd proceeded against according to law, and he was brought to trial at the Old Bailey, in 1701, for murder and piracy upon the high seas.

At the same time, the House of Commons was proceeding upon an impeachment of the Earl of Oxford and Lord Somers, for certain high crimes and misdemeanors, one of which was their connection with Kidd, and their agency in passing the commissions and grant to him, as prejudicial to public service and private trade, and dishonorable to the King, contrary to the law of England and to the Bill of Rights. It was urged in reply that a pirate was hostis humani generis, and his goods belonged to whomsoever it might be that destroyed him, and the King granted title only to that for which no owner was to be found. Before the lords were acquitted Bellomont was dead, and Kidd was hung; while popular feeling ran high, parties took sides in the affair; there were accusations afloat that these lords, now on their own trial, had set the Great Seal of England to the pardon of the arch-pirate; and as the anti-Ministerial side was determined to hang Kidd in order to prove the complicity and guilt of the Ministers with him, the Ministers themselves were, of course, determined to hang him to prove their own innocence.

Kidd made a very good appearance upon his trial, ignorant as he was of all the forms of law; he insisted on his innocence, and that he had only captured ships with French passes or sailing under the French flag, and he fought manfully, but to no purpose. Of the men that were tried with him, several plead that they surrendered themselves upon a certain proclamation of the King's pardon, but the Court decided that, not having surrendered themselves to the designated persons, they did not come within its provisions, and they must swing for it, and so they did. A couple of servants were acquitted; but to Kidd himself no mercy was shown. Justice Turton, Dr. Newton, Advocate for the Admiralty, and the Lord Chief Baron, all made elaborate arguments against him, while no one spoke for him; and all his previous plunderings were allowed to be cited in the Court, in order to prove that he plundered the Quedagh Merchant. When he desired to have counsel assigned him, Sir Salathiel Lovell, the Recorder, wonderingly asks him, "What would you have counsel for?" And Dr. Oxenden contemptuously inquires, "What matter of law can you have?" But as Kidd quietly answers, "There be matters of law, my lord," the Recorder asks again, "Mr. Kidd, do you know what you mean by matters of law?" Whereupon Kidd replies as quietly as before, "I know what I mean; I desire to put off my trial as long as I can, till I can get my evidence ready." He has had but a fortnight's notice of his trial, and knowing how important a delay would be to him in which the popular feeling might die out or abate, he urges, "I beg your lordships' patience till I can procure my papers. I had a couple of French passes, which I must make use of to my justification," and presently adds, "I beg your lordships I may have counsel admitted, and that my trial may be put off; I am not really prepared for it." To which the Recorder rudely replies, "Nor never will, if you can help it."

Kidd still contended for counsel, and at last it was assigned to him. It then appeared that he had already petitioned for money to carry on his trial, and though it had, as a matter of course, been granted to him, as to any prisoner, it had been put into his hands only on the night before. His counsel, for whose services he had so exerted himself, made one or two timid remarks, but, after the jury were sworn, although the Solicitor-General plied the witnesses with leading questions, the cowardly lawyers never cross-examined, made any plea, or opened their lips.

The indictment for murder, upon which Kidd was first tried, portrayed, with great particularity, the blow struck the gunner, saying that of that mortal bruise "the aforesaid William Moore, from the thirtieth day of October * * * until the one-and-thirtieth day * * * did

languish, and languishing did live," but on the one-and-thirtieth day did die, and declaring that William Kidd feloniously, voluntarily and of malice aforethought did kill and murder him; to all of which Kidd plead not guilty, constantly interrupting the Court with his exclamations and explanations. "The passes were seized by my Lord Bellomont; that we will prove as clear as the day!" cries he. When invited to find cause for exception in the jury, he either adroitly or ingenuously answers, "I shall challenge none; I know nothing to the contrary but they are honest men." The time coming for his defense, he told in an earnest manner a short and simple story, but one in which, by comparison of the various witnesses, several discrepancies with the truth were found. "My lord," said he, "I will tell you what the case was. I was coming up within a league of the Dutchman, and some of my men were making a mutiny about taking her, and my gunner told the people he could put the captain in a way to take the ship and be safe. Says I, 'How will you do that?' The gunner answered, 'We will get the captain and men aboard.' 'And what then?' 'We will go aboard the ship and plunder her, and we will have it under their hands that we did not take her.' Says I, 'This is Judas-like. I dare not do such a thing.' Says he, 'We may do it, we are beggars already.' 'Why,' says I, 'may we take this ship because we are poor?' Upon that a mutiny arose, so I took up a bucket and just throwed it at him, and said, 'You are a rogue to make such a motion.' This I can prove, my lord."

But he did not prove it, and though he struggled hard to do so, and though his faithful servant Richard Barlicorn, also on trial for his life, must have committed a hundred perjuries in his behalf, the Court could not find evidence of any mutiny for more than a month before the gunner's death, and decided that William Moore's outcry that Kidd had brought him and many others to ruin was not sufficient provocation for the killing. And though Kidd plead that striking the man in a passion, with so rude and unpremeditated a weapon as the first slush-bucket at hand, if not justifiable as a preventive of mutiny, was, at furthest, no more than manslaughter, and exclaimed that "it was not designedly done, but in his passion, for which he was heartily sorry," yet, it being determined to hang him at all odds, the lawyers were given hints, the witnesses were browbeaten, and the jury were instructed, after tedious iteration, to bring him in guilty; which was done.

At the trial next day on the indictments for piracy, Kidd did not lose heart. There were but two important witnesses produced against him, Palmer, one of his crew, and his ship's surgeon, Bradinham, who, though both of them sharers in his adventures, had become evidence for the Crown on the promise of their own safety. Kidd himself cross-questioned them, but idly, their replies being always straightforward and consistent. His only defense was that he had taken French passes from every capture, that the Earl of Bellomont had seized them, and that his men, once catching sight of a French pass when a ship was overhauled, would not let that ship go, and for the rest answered, with indifference, "That is what these witnesses say," as if such depraved testimony could really be worth nothing. "Did you hear me say so !" he demanded of Palmer once. "I heard you say so," was the reply. "I am sure," said Kidd then, contemptuously, "you never heard me say such a word to such a loggerhead as you." But matters going beyond his patience soon, "Hear me !" he cried indignantly, but was silenced by the Court, only to break out again presently on Palmer with, "Certainly you have not the impudence to say that !" and to adjure him to "speak true." By-and-by the question of one of the passes being up, "Palmer, did you see that pass ?" he eagerly asks ; and, the old subordinate manner returning to the other man, he answers, "Indeed, captain, I did not ;" whereupon, like one who throws up his hands in despair, Kidd exclaims, "What boots it to ask him any questions ? We have no witnesses, and what we say signifies nothing." With Bradinham he is less contemptuous and more enraged. "This man contradicts himself in a hundred places !" he declared. "He tells a thousand lies * * * There was no such thing in November ; he knows no more of these things than you do. This fellow used to sleep five or six months together in the hold ! * * * It is hard," he exclaims after awhile, "that a couple of rascals should take away the King's subjects' lives. Because I did not turn pirate, you rogues, you would make me one !" And, with that, hope slips faster and faster away from his grasp, and when the Solicitor-General would know if he has anything further to ask of the witnesses, he replies, "No, no ! So long as he swears it, our words or oaths cannot be taken. No, no," he

continues, wearily, "it signifies nothing." But he does ask at last one other question. "Mr. Bradinham," he cries, bitterly, "are not you promised your life to take away mine ?" and a little later he adds, with dignity, "I will not trouble the Court any more, for it is a folly," and when the final word of the Judge has been uttered, that he shall be taken thence to his execution, he says, "My lord, it is a very hard sentence. For my part, I am the innocentest person of them all, only I have been sworn against by perjured persons."

The feeling against Kidd, though, was hardly satisfied even by his death ; and fearful lest they had lost a victim, after all, the public circulated stories of his escape, and of the hanging of a man of straw in his place, although if the "blunt monster with uncounted heads" had taken the trouble to use one of those heads, the absurdity of the rumor might have been evident; for Kidd's evil fortune pursued him even from the scaffold, and the rope breaking, doubled and prolonged the last awful moments, and between the first hanging and the final one he was heard to have conversation with the executioner, ere passing to that Bar where he was judged, let us hope, after a different fashion.

But the death of Captain Kidd put an end to piracy in the American and most other seas ; and, in the meantime, so far from lying concealed to enrich the poor treasure-seekers of our coasts, all the gains of Captain Kidd, illgotten at the best, have gone to swell the revenues of the English Kingdom.

CHARLESTOWN.

The traveler who seeks the cool northeast seaside is scarcely aware how near it is to him when, after his wearisome journey, he crosses the narrow and crooked streets which are Boston's crown of picturesque glory, and leaves the city by the Eastern Railway. For no sooner has the train moved out of the station than the sea-views begin to open on him as he goes—vistas of the broad, blue bay; streams just emptying in; salt marshes, rich with every tint and every odor; the bold bluffs of Nahant; the long lines and lonely houses of the Chelsea beaches; forts far away in the harbor, where the flag waves like a blossom on its reed; and town after town, all more or less historic, and all full of the wild sea-breath that gives such a bloom to the faces of their women, and such a vigor to their men. He has hardly crossed the first bridge before one of these towns rises on his sight, sitting on her hill the while as fair as any pictured city of walls and towers, and overlooking the Mystic and the Charles, and the wide and windy bay. Indeed, a lovelier view of any town I do not know than Charlestown, when seen from the car window, her lights reflected in the water at her feet, and her streets lifted in tier over tier, till the lofty spire of the hill-top church glitters in the moon or starlight far above them all.

It is not so charming a spot, however, upon nearer acquaintance, for most of its streets are as narrow as those of the neighboring metropolis, and not one-half so clean, and it is more interesting as a congregation of workshops, foundries, and great industrial establishments, than in any other light; for, owing to the circumstance of five towns having been set off from it, and a part of four others, it has now the smallest territory of any town in the State of Massachusetts, and is necessarily crowded. Running along the waterside is the Navy Yard, surrounded by a massive granite wall, ten feet high, and encircling the barracks both for marines and officers and their families, together with the great machine-shops, ropewalks, shipyards, wharves, dry-docks, and other Government works on a vast scale, thronged with two thousand busy artisans, and all guarded by sentries pacing their perpetual round, and by the receiving-ship Ohio, anchored in the stream beyond. This whole agglomeration of men and trades forms a strong political element in its locality, and a prominent and potential member of Congress has been heard to declare that he once staid six weeks in Washington after the session in order to secure the appointment of a common painter in the Navy Yard, and failed at last.

The State Prison, another lion of the place, is a machine hardly less powerful, as any one might easily imagine who saw it entrenched behind its perpendicular fortifications and rows of spikes, and thought of the number of officials necessary to carry on its operations and maintain order among its unhappy denizens. It is a gloomy-looking fabric, like all the traditional prisons "that slur the sunshine half a mile," and a satirist has mentioned the fact as characteristic of certain inconsistencies between theory and practice common in Massachusetts, that almost the only place within her borders where a liberty-cap is displayed is at the top of her State Prison, not so glaring an inconsistency, nevertheless, as it at first sight appears, since the imprisonment of criminals means the freedom of all the rest of society.

In quite another portion of Charlestown stands the famous Bunker Hill Monument, making the most attractive feature of the town, with its gray shaft rising in perfect symmetry from the ample space at the summit of a lofty and smoothly-swarded green hill. Here the statue of Warren is to be found, with various trophies of the Revolution, less interesting in themselves than are the suggestions of the scene—a scene that calls up one morning, almost a hundred years ago, with the unquailing farmers gathered behind their breastworks of sod and hay, and the flashing bayonets and scarlet lines of British grenadiers moving up the hill, while the town below was blazing in a conflagration of every dwelling there; that calls up another morning fifty years later, where trembling old hands, that, when youth and chivalry were at flood, helped to lay the corner-stone of the Republic, now in the midst of its success laid the corner-stone of this monument to one of its first struggles for existence, and, in the presence of the survivors of that struggle, the thunders of Webster's eloquence were answered by the thunders of the people's applause. Who is it that declares the inclosure at Bunker Hill peculiarly typical of our national characteristics, inasmuch as, being badly beaten there, we built a monument to the fact, and have never ceased boasting thereof? One thing can certainly be said in reply, that the moral effect in teaching the enemy how sadly in earnest the brave rebels were, and in encouraging the dispirited patriots by sight of raw recruits thrice breaking the form of the invading veterans, was something inestimable; that rail fence stuffed with meadow-hay was not merely the breastwork of Putnam and Prescott, it was the first redoubt of freedom the wide world over, and from Bunker Hill began that march of noble thought and grand action across this continent which is destined to overthrow all tyrannies, both of intellect and of empire, in this hemisphere to-day, to-morrow in the other. It gives one a very satisfactory emotion of patriotism to stand on Bunker Hill, as well as a good idea of the recuperative power of the country, for when the enemy drove every soul out of Charlestown, and burned every building there, it was but five hundred houses in all that were destroyed, while to-day the population approaches the number of forty thousand. It is a population, however, that must have undergone many changes; as, for instance, one would fancy that its action of thirty years ago, in the destruction of the Ursuline Convent, would, at present, be quite impossible, since the Catholic Church now far outnumbers any other single sect in the place—for the Catholic Church has a subtle, self-healing way with it like that belonging to some natural organism, so that where it has received a wound, thither it immediately sends its best and freshest blood to repair the harm, as the case is with the limb of an animal or the branch of a tree, and thus mending itself and growing with greater vigor where the hurt was, it presently outstrips injury, and plants itself in the place of its assailant.

The Ursuline Convent just mentioned belonged, at the time of its demolition, to one of the congregations of Ursulines founded some three hundred years earlier as a religious sisterhood for nursing the sick, relieving and instructing the poor, and named for the martyred St. Ursula, a Christian princess of Britain, and one of the first to associate maidens with herself for devout purposes. Originally every Sister remained in her own home, and performed from that point such duties as were hers; but shortly after the death of Angela Merici, the foundress, they adopted a uniform dress, their principles and plan of action became more widely spread, and they gradually gathered together under the same roof, chose a Directress, or Superior, and took some simple vows, vows afterward exchanged for others of a more solemn nature. In the year 1860 there were more than five hundred houses of Ursulines in the world; and, never entirely abandoning their original purpose, they are to-day principally devoted to the tuition and care of young girls; and of such benefit to the general community have they always been considered, that, when certain European Governments put an end to the existence of convents within their territory, the Ursulines were permitted to remain unmolested, and were moreover aided and encouraged in their work. The ruins of the Ursuline Convent in Charlestown stand in a remote part of the town, lately taken into the village of Somerville, on a place known as Mount Benedict, and smoke-blackened and weather-beaten, the broken walls and chimneys have stood for more than thirty years till becoming picturesque with time. Wild cherry trees have sprung up within the walls of the cloisters, and have grown into full bearing of their bitter fruit; cattle browse among them, and lie beneath the great trees that have arched themselves, untaught, over the old avenues; sheep crop the turf where once the nuns' flower-garden may have been, and where, long since, the natural growth of the place has retaken its own rights, and where here and there a weed blooms, which is only a garden-flower returned to its one original stock. One side of the hill commands the harbor and the placid Charles, with a view of the neighboring metropolis, just remote enough for a haze of distance to render it poetic; and on the other side, far away across meadows and bending elms, the blue and lovely Mystic winds to the sea, and soft, low hills inclose the wide and varied landscape. It is a retreat of peace, that now remains unbroken by anything except the rudeness of the winter storms, but it bears upon it the moss-grown marks of a violence sadly in contrast, for thirty-five years ago it was the scene of an outrage on human rights and freedom of thought, which, it is to be hoped, neither this country nor this age shall behold again. The convent had been founded in 1820 by Doctors Matignon and Cheverus with funds contributed for that purpose by a resident and native of the city of Boston; and upon their urgency a few Sisters of the Ursuline Order came to this country, and made Boston their home. The confinement and the city air, however, disturbed their health, accustomed as they had been to the out-door exercise of their gardens, and, some half-dozen years after their arrival, the bishop procured for them the estate in Charlestown, to which they immediately removed, occupying a farmhouse at the foot of the hill till their own residence upon the summit should be completed. This was done in the next year, and it was shortly so crowded with pupils from New England, the West Indies, Southern States and British provinces, that a couple of years afterward two large wings were added to the establishment, the number of nuns varying from four to ten, and the pupils from fifty to sixty.

The feeling in Charlestown toward them could hardly ever have been of a hospitable nature, for one of the Selectmen of the town, who appears to have been of a very inflammable temperament, told the Superior that it had been his intention on the first night of the occupancy of the farmhouse by the nuns to come with thirty men and tear it down about their ears, but he was deterred by the quiet procession of the little company taking their walks across the hill next day, which appears to have been a moving sight to him. Welcome or not, however, the school prospered wonderfully, as indeed it could hardly help doing when the teachers were so devoted to their duties, the fact of their being devoted for life being probably the chief secret of their success. There was then comparatively little attention paid to science and the severer studies generally, and the education of women was confined almost especially to the accomplishments of language, music, and painting, which were taught here to perfection; and, thronged with pupils and applicants, it is possible the school aroused the jealousy of those who conjectured the good income which it yearly added to the revenues of a Church they abominated. There was no need, though, of adding this jealousy to the elements at work in the neighborhood already distrustful of Roman Catholic institutions, keeping a vigilant lookout over what it considered as little less than a branch of the Inquisition introduced into the midst of it, constantly fearful of Catholic supremacy—not from any largeness of view concerning the Church as a Church of authority denying the right of individual opinion, and thus a drag upon the wheels of progress, but with an imagination inflamed by the wood-cuts of "Fox's Book of Martyrs," by such legends as that old one of the unfaithful nun, sealed up alive in a wall, and regarding the quiet building on the hill not as a place of innocent merriment and girlish study, but of severe penance, of horrible punishment, of underground cells and passages through which all the mighty power of the Church walked abroad to crush any refractory spirit into death or submission. There were sad rumors of barbarities exercised upon the sick, of a child sent away in an advanced stage of scarlet-fever, of fearful penances imposed upon a dying nun. It was also urged that the Convent made great effort to secure the children of Protestants for proselyting purposes, excluding the children of Catholics; oblivious of the truth that its doors were open to all who were able to meet the cost of such expensive education, that, its pupils being chiefly daughters of the wealthy, there really belonged to Catholic parents a proportion of them corresponding to the proportion of wealthy Catholics in the community at large, while for poorer Catholics a free school already existed in Boston, where their education was provided for quite suitably to their probable station in life; and in the meantime not a single pupil, in all the number educated in the convent, had ever become a nun, nor had one even been converted to Catholicism. But more than this inherited dread of papacy and its influence were the swarms of suspicions of another sort. It makes one doubtful of the inherent worth of human nature to hear the baseness of conjecture indulged in by these people; it seems as if they were so vile themselves that they could believe in the virtue of no others; because priests assumed to be celibate and nuns to be virgin, they denounced the good bishop as a monster and the stainless Sisters as prodigies of impurity. And as time wore on, and all these unfortunate feelings and fancies glowed more and more hotly, it needed but a single spark to kindle the flame of intolerance into open action among this population, watchful, and ready to give the worst possible construction to every simple circumstance.

The flame was kindled quickly enough. In the summer of 1834 there were fifty-four young girls, from all parts of the country, students in the convent, and ten nuns resident there—two of the latter being novices, and therefore doing nothing in the schoolroom. Of these fifty-four young girls, it is probable that nearly all took music-lessons, while there appear to have been but two of the nuns attending to music—one of these an invalid already in consumption—so that the greater part of the hundred and odd music-lessons a week fell to the share of the other—Sister Mary John, formerly, when in the world and retaining the name of her birth, a Miss Elizabeth Harrison. Miss Harrison was a native of Philadelphia, had passed her novitiate of two years, and had for four years been a member in full communion. She had a brother and a brother-in-law living in Boston, across the bridge, and visiting her at the convent whenever they chose; and as she had, besides, unrestricted opportunities of reposing confidence in her pupils, had she desired to be taken from the convent nothing would have been easier—all the more as no restraint was put upon an individual there; and two nuns who had taken the vail had left, without let or hindrance, and still maintained friendly relations with the Superior. She had been giving steadily fourteen lessons a day of forty-five minutes each; any one who has studied or taught music, or who has been present during a lesson in that art, knows what an exquisitely trying thing to the nerves it is, and Miss Harrison was not only tired and weak, but her brain was in a state of high excitement. Several members of her family had been subject to occasional mental alienation—a circumstance of which had the Ursulines been aware upon her reception among them, they would probably have allotted her less fatiguing duties. Old Dr. Warren had already pronounced Miss Harrison's health to be very delicate; always in excessively cold or warm weather she had trouble in her head, and feeling this quite badly, at about the last of July, she had foolishly taken an emetic which had acted strangely with her; she began to manifest great restlessness, went about the house acting extravagantly, clamoring for new instruments, setting the doors wide open as if to cool her fever, and when, one afternoon, the Superior told her that she looked too ill to be attending to the lessons, she replied by a burst of laughter, and her nervous excitement culminating in delirium as the heat of the day increased, she slipped out of the convent, into the grounds, and away to a neighbor's house, unobserved by the Sisters, who would never have dreamed of such a thing, as she was a person incapable of disguising her feelings, and had never before been heard to express the least dissatisfaction, but of whom, on the contrary, it was thought that there could not be a happier person than she in the whole Ursuline Order. From the neighbor's house she was taken by the Selectman, himself another neighbor, and the one who had at first intended to tear down the farmhouse about the nuns' ears, to the residence of a gentleman in West Cambridge, after which, going to the convent, he notified the Superior of what he had done, and on the next day the brother of the young lady went to see her. Probably the rest from her labors and the change of scene had already acted beneficially on Miss Harrison's mind, for she implored her brother to bring Bishop Fenwick to her, as if she longed for his assistance in regaining her self-control. It would seem that the bishop had been disinclined to interfere; but, on the solicitation of the Superior, he went with Miss Harrison's brother in the afternoon to visit her. Bishop Fenwick testified upon oath that he found Miss Harrison in a state of derangement, her looks haggard, her expressions incoherent, while she laughed and cried in the same moment ; that his one object in going for her was to take her to the convent, clothe her properly, and send her to her friends, presuming that she left because dissatisfied with her mode of treatment ; but when he proposed her return to her home, she begged and entreated to be allowed to remain. Upon her restoration to the convent, she declared that "she did not know what it all meant," and she begged the people who called upon her not to refer any more to the circumstances of her brief absence, for she could not be responsible for what she then said or did. To Miss Alden, who in past times had heard her frequently say that she could never cease to be thankful

enough for having been called to that happy state of life, and who now visited her, she expressed the greatest horror at the step she had taken, and said that she would prefer death to leaving. And upon being examined in court, on the trial of the rioters, she averred that had any one ever told her she should do what she had done, she would have thought it impossible ; that nothing was omitted, in the conduct of the institution, that could contribute to her happiness or to that of the other inmates ; that her recollection of what took place after her flight was very indistinct, for she was bereft of reason ; and she covered her face and burst into tears.

The worst conjecture, one would have

ESCAPE OF THE "MYSTERIOUS LADY" FROM THE URSULINE CONVENT OF MT. BENEDICT.—"HER NERVOUS EXCITEMENT CULMINATING IN DELIRIUM, SHE SLIPPED OUT OF THE CONVENT."

thought, that, in uncharity, could have been put upon this affair, would have been that, never of very strong mind, and now worn out with the unceasing recurrence of her labors, she had suddenly imagined the life unbearable, and in a wild moment had escaped from it only to find herself grown unused to the world, and more unhappy there than over her old tasks in the convent. But that was truth beside the calumnies that instantly sprang into being upon the foundation of this unfortunate occurrence. It was remembered, too, that another young woman had left Mount Benedict not long previously, and the atrocious slanders upon the sisterhood which she scattered wherever she went were revived with added burden, and there was hardly any scandal possible to be invented but was repeated and believed, till the stately brick edifice on the hill was honestly regarded far and near, by the bigoted and narrow-minded of the untaught population, as a den of wickedness and filth; and a conspiracy for its suppression was hurriedly formed, not only in Charlestown, but throughout other towns and extending into other States. Matters probably were greatly hastened then by the appearance in one of the neighboring newspapers of a paragraph entitled "The Mysterious Lady," and containing the items of local gossip about Miss Harrison's escapade, magnified and exaggerated into the flight of a nun brought back by force, and either murdered, secreted in the underground vaults, or sent away for some awful punishment in remoter regions; and this was only the visible and audible expression of what appears to have been in the minds of nearly all, if not in their mouths; and the first manner in which the general feeling outcropped was by waylaying the convent-gardener and beating him within an inch of his life, wreaking in a vicarious way the vengeance that could not yet arrive at his employers.

A few days after Miss Harrison's return to Mount Benedict, the Lady Superior, whom Dr. Thompson, a Charlestown physician, has mentioned as "thoroughly educated, dignified in her person, and elegant in her manners, pure in her morals, of generous and magnanimous feelings, and of high religious principles," was rude y waited on by one of the Selectmen of the town—the same whose kind intentions respecting the farmhouse have been mentioned—and informed that the convent would be destroyed if the Mysterious Lady could not be seen. The Superior had already told this gentleman the state of Miss Harrison's health, and the incidents leading to her temporary aberration of mind, and she knew it was quite in his power to contradict any wrong impression abroad, and to quell any uneasiness without troubling her further; but, it being Sunday, she now appointed Monday, the next day, for the five Selectmen to be shown over the establishment, and included in her invitation two neighbors who had been instrumental in increasing the popular prejudice. On Monday the visitors came, and ferreted the house through from cellar to cupola, occupying three hours, looking even into the paint-boxes, searching every closet, opening every drawer, assisted by the Mysterious Lady, Miss Harrison, herself, in person. Their errand done, they declared themselves satisfied that not only was there nothing to censure in the least, but, on the other hand, much to praise, and they adjourned to the house

of one of their number to prepare a pronunciamento to that purpose for the morning papers. They had but little more than left the building, just before sunset, when a group of men gathered about the gates of the avenue, using impertinent language, but, upon the Superior's notifying the Selectmen, she was assured there was not the least prospect of the occurrence of anything disagreeable. It was shortly after nine in the evening when she became more seriously alarmed by a great noise on the Medford road, made by an advancing mob, with cries of "Down with the convent! Down with the convent!" With much presence of mind, she instantly aroused the Community, telling them she feared they were in danger—the rioters on the road, meanwhile, constantly increasing in force with new arrivals, on foot and in wagons, from every quarter. After waking those that were asleep, she went into the second story of the building, and, throwing up a window, asked the party of forty or fifty gathered outside what they desired, adding that they were disturbing the slumbers of the pupils, some of whom were the children of their most respected fellow-citizens. They replied that they did not mean to hurt the children, but they must see the nun that had run away. The Superior went to fetch her, but found that she had fainted with fright, and lay insensible in the arms of four of the Sisters. The Superior then returned to tell the people that this was the case; she asserted to them that the establishment had that day been visited by the Selectmen, who had been pleased with all they saw, and would assure them of it, and that if they would call on the next day, at a suitable hour, they should have every satisfaction. They asked her if she were protected, and she answered, "Yes, by legions!" invoking the celestial guardians. But other parties having come to swell their numbers, they replied in indecent terms, calling her an old figurehead made of brass, telling her that she was lying, and that they had one of the Selectmen with them who had opened the gates to them. The Selectman then came forward, and advised the Superior to throw herself on his protection, but as he was the same Selectman whose officiousness had already produced much of the trouble, the Superior, after asking him if he had secured the attendance of any other members of the board, refused to trust her establishment to his safe-keeping, telling him, if he wished to befriend her, first to disperse the mob. This he feebly attempted, deterring the rioters from firing the building, when they called for torches, by telling them that if lights were brought they would be recognized and detected—after which noble effort he returned to his house, and valiantly went to bed.

The mob then fired a gun in the labyrinth under the willow-trees, possibly as a token of some sort to their accomplices, and withdrew a little, while waiting for the fresh arrivals. At about eleven o'clock the fences were torn up and a bonfire kindled, which is believed to have been a concerted signal for the presence of all the conspirators, and the bells being rung as for an alarm of fire, both in Charlestown and Boston, multitudes pressed to the spot. Several fire-engines also appeared—the Charlestown ones halting opposite the bonfire, and one from Boston passing up to the front of the mansion, where it was seized upon by the mob and prevented from doing any service when needed, if so inclined. Rumor still runs that at this point, when Boston would have sent other engines and further means to subdue the disturbance, the drawbridges were lifted, and it was found to be impossible to get them down. The arrival of the engine from Boston was, however, instantly followed by an assault upon the building in the shape of a shower of brick-bats and clubs again-t the windows, after which the bold assailants waited to see if any defense was to be made, or any resentment manifested to this attack, which they knew might kill' or maim many of the helpless inmates. This brief pause allowed the Lady Superior opportunity to marshal her little flock, whom she had refused previously to allow to leave the building, lest that should be only betraying it to its destruction, and under convoy of the terrified Sisters to secure their retreat down the garden, into the summer-house, and over the fence into the adjoining grounds, where they were safe till they could be collected in a friendly house: there had been sixty children to be taken care of, and of the nuns that night one was in the last stages of pulmonary consumption, one was in convulsive fits, and Miss Harrison had been wrought, by the agitation of the evening, to a raving delirium. The Superior, having performed this duty, lingered herself, with the true spirit of a leader in such situation, opening the doors of every room and looking into every dormitory, calling every child by name, to be sure that none were left behind, and then, last of all, descending to her own room to secure the valuables there, together with a thousand dollars belonging to the revenue of the institution; but before the last of the children had left the building the varlets had poured in, and as she herself fled from it they were but ten feet behind her. In a moment afterward the house was filled with the mob, shouting, yelling, and blaspheming; torches snatched from the engines lighted the way for them, they ransacked every room, rifled every trunk, broke open every drawer, stole watches, thrust the costly jewelry of the Spanish children into their pockets, split up the piano-fortes, shattered the splendid harps, and even made way with the altar ornaments presented by the good Archbishop of Bordeaux. Having satisfied their curiosity and greed, they piled up the furniture, curtains, books, pictures, in the centre of the several rooms, and deliberately set fire to every heap, threw in the altar vestments, the Bible and the cross, and, the act of virtue consummated, left the building in flames. After this, the bishop's lodge experienced a similar fate, the farmhouse belonging to the institute followed, and the grand demonstration of proper religious sentiment wound up with tearing open the tomb of the place, pillaging the sacred vessels there, stealing the coffin-plates, and scattering the ashes of the dead to the four winds.

Not a hand was lifted to stay these abominable proceedings, by any one of the vast multitude outside; the firemen, who declared frequently that they could prevent the flames if allowed, were hindered from acting—although their sincerity may be suspected from the fact that an engine returned to Boston decked with the flowers stolen from the altar; the magistrates neither made any remonstrance, nor read the riot-act, nor demanded help of neigh-

LEGEND OF CHARLESTOWN.

RUINS OF THE URSULINE CONVENT OF MT. BENEDICT.

boring towns, nor asked for the services of the marines at the Navy Yard, nor made a single arrest during all the seven hours of the riot. And though the outside multitude, who took no part in the crime, were all Protestants, not one of them dared to protest against this outrage, not only upon weakness and defencelessness, but upon civil liberty, and all remained paralyzed until the end, doubtful perhaps if there were enough disapprovers among them to be of any avail, and entirely forgetful that a stream from a single engine-hose would have dispersed the whole mob more quickly than a battery could have done.

Meanwhile the nuns, escaping with difficulty, and with yet greater difficulty supporting the young consumptive, Sister Mary St. Henry, and getting her across the fence at the garden's foot, had found a kindly shelter, and were shortly afterward invited by old General Dearborn to his seat in Roxbury, called Brinley Place, where they found once more a home, although, before they were fairly settled there, Mary St. Henry died, at the age of twenty. Though an invalid, this young woman had been able to give a lesson on the day of the destruction of the convent; all that night she lay in a cold rigor, and eleven days afterward she was dead. Her funeral was one of unusual pomp; every Catholic in the vicinity made an object of attending, half the citizens of Boston were organized into a special police through expectation of some requital, and so deeply roused were the feelings of the injured party, that it is probable nothing but the most unremitting exertions of their clergy prevented severe retaliation. The matter, however, did not end here immediately. Loud expressions of disapprobation were heard from all portions of the State, and a self-constituted Committee, of the best names in Boston, including such as Robert C. Winthrop, William Appleton, Horace Mann, Theophilus Parsons, and Thomas Motley, prepared at once to investigate the affair, and bring, if possible, the miscreants to justice. They examined more than one hundred and forty persons, and, chiefly by their exertions, thirteen arrests were made, of which eight were of a capital nature. The young woman who had scattered the atrocious slanders was visited, and she retracted everything but the assertions relative to the severe penances of the sick nun; but even on that point her word was discredited by means of other witnesses, the sisters by birth of Mary St. Henry; it was proved that she had been a charity-student in the institute, desirous of taking the vail, admitted on probation for six months to discover if she had either capacity, sincerity, or strength of character, failing to display which she was about to be dismissed, when she left secretly. Miss Alden, a young lady who had taken the white vail at Mount Benedict, and afterward freely left it, testified that, upon living there two years, she became convinced that she had no vocation for an ascetic life, and made her feelings known to the Superior, who advised her accordingly, strongly as they were attached to each other, to depart if she could not be happy there, of which no one could judge but herself, and to her decision it should be left, for their rules allowed no one to remain except such as found their happiness there, and there only. "She told me," said Miss Alden, "that I was at liberty to go when I pleased, and should be provided with everything requisite for my departure—which was done two years after, having remained that length of time merely from personal attachment to the Lady Superior." And, it was equally evident that others desiring to do so had been allowed to separate themselves from the Community in the same manner. The charge of inhumanity to the sick was also sifted, and found amounting to nothing; the child with the scarlet-fever having been sent home upon the first symptom of the disease, to prevent the infection's reaching the remaining children. And to an assertion in relation to secret vaults beneath the building, the mason, one Peter Murphy, who laid the foundations, declared, under his own signature, that nothing of the kind existed. Although unanimously opposed to the Roman Catholic forms of religion, the Committee published a most magnanimous report of their investigation ; and finally a man by the name of Buzzell was brought to trial as a ringleader in the late atrocity. He received, however, a very singular trial ; one of the jurymen was several times

seen to be asleep ; and though it was proved to be he that had beaten the convent-gardener, that had been seen actively encouraging the rioters, breaking the doors, bringing tar-barrels and firing them, and though on the retirement of the jury they stood seven to five for conviction, on the way from their room to the court-room they became unanimous for acquittal. The only person ever punished for complicity in the affair, was a mere boy, convicted on very insufficient evidence, but for whom it was probably supposed the penalty would be made right ; he was sentenced to imprisonment for life, his mother died of a broken heart, and finally he was pardoned out, ruined, and old before his time. There all proceedings ended. The nuns were invited to establish themselves at Newport, in the land where Roger Williams made religious toleration a fact, but the proposition was declined, partly perhaps because the attack showed where their work was needed, and partly in the belief that Massachusetts would render justice, inasmuch as having always paid for protection, when then the protection was withheld the State became responsible for all damages. This responsibility has never been met. Repayment has been constantly urged by all denominations ; Theodore Parker made himself especially prominent in the matter ; but, owing to a mistaken judgment of what the popular opinion may be, no Legislature has yet been found with sufficient courage to make an appropriation to reimburse the Convent for its losses, and in refusing this demand for payment the State has virtually repeated the outrage year by year.

Perhaps no more scathing commentary on the whole matter will ever be made than that to be found in the following exact copy :

"November 26, 1834.

"Received of Bishop Fenwick, the sum of seventy-nine dollars and twenty cents, the same being taxes assessed by the Assessors of the town of Charlestown, upon the land and buildings of the late Convent of Mount Benedict, for the year 1834, and which were this day demanded by Solomon Hovey, Jr., Collector, agreeably to instructions received by him from the Assessors, to that effect, although said buildings had been destroyed by a mob in August last.

"$79.20.   (Signed)

"Solomon Hovey, Jr., Collector."

SALEM.

When the traveler loses sight of Charlestown, with its twin but incongruous monuments, his train is passing out on the meadows dotted with haycocks and alive with every tint of red and russet, and presently is skirting the shores of Swampscot and Lynn. Here, perhaps, he glances up at the High Rock commanding sight of the dim line of the Beverley beaches, of the Cape Ann Shadows, the jagged coast of Marblehead, the long sweep of the Swampscot sands, the wild cliffs of Nahant, and the immense horizon of the bay beyond— a spot where Moll Pitcher for so many years performed her mysteries ; and twenty minutes afterward the train is running into a region where witch and warlock, once holding revel, still haunt every inch of the ground. This region, whose centre is known as the town of Salem, is very lovely in the river-banks and villas of its outskirts. For the town itself, slight marks remain of the old Puritan domination, and its days of East Indian glory and spicy argosies are over. Reminiscences of that glory, however, continue to give caste in the place, and every lady in Salem has a cachemire shawl, it is said, or else has no passport to society ; and great warehouses and great fortunes remain to tell of the state that has passed away. Among the smaller towns along the coast, Salem is still the most wealthy, and is therefore the target for much ill-nature on the part of her poorer neighbors. Nothing equals the contempt which a Lynn man feels for a citizen of Salem, unless it is the contempt which a Gloucester man feels, or that which a Salem man not only feels but manifests, for both of the others and the rest of creation besides. In Marblehead this hostility reaches more open expression, and the mutual sentiments of both populations are uttered by the urchins there when they cry : "Here comes a Salem boy—let's rock him round the corner !" Nevertheless, Salem contrives to creep along, to found her museum, to become headquarters for the Essex Institute, and to make herself, in ever so slight a measure, a centre of culture and advance. Lately the Scientific Societies met there, and were—undreamed-of thing—invited home to dinner : in a town where, if necessity obliges you to call upon a man at his club, he comes out and shuts the door behind him, keeping a grasp upon the handle as an intimation of the brevity of your visit—where Choate and Webster, pleading in court, have picked up a luncheon, at noontide, in hotel or eating-house, as best they might, and where Hawthorne all but starved. Salem is conspicuous among New England towns for the beauty of its women ; a plain face would be an anomaly there, and the well-fed blood of wealthy generations is told by the bloomy skins and abundant tresses, the expression of sweetness and dignity, the soft eyes and fine features, of the daughters of the place. The town still preserves a few relics of its memorable past ; the House of the Seven Gables was standing there a little while ago, together with the Townsend-Bishop house, famous for its share in the old witchcraft transactions, and the Corwin house, at the corner of North and Essex streets, where the Grand Jury sat upon those transactions. There are some handsome churches and public buildings of more modern date, and a stone Court-house, together with a fine Registry of Deeds. There is an interest attaching to this latter structure, not altogether archæological though concerning itself with antiquities, but an interest in one of the darkest problems ever presented by human nature ; for here are kept such documents as have been preserved from the witchcraft days, and among them the death-warrant of Bridget Bishop. Very few indeed are these papers ; for, when the frenzy of the period began to subside, those "Salem Gentlemen" who petitioned the Government to grant no reprieve to Rebecca Nurse, a woman who had lived nearly eighty years of a saintly life, were overtaken by remorse and shame, and hastened to do away with all remembrance of their recent action, exhibiting a better sense of the fitness of things than their descendants do who to-day display in a sealed vial a dozen bent and verdigrised and rusty pins purporting to be the identical ones with which their forefathers plagued the witches ; albeit, it is said, the fashion of these pins was not known at the time when those poor wretches were tormented. Indeed to the stranger in the town witchcraft is the one thought ; he looks at these people whom he meets upon the street, and they become to him curious subjects of conjecture as he reflects that intermarriage has obliterated the ancient feud and rancor, and wonders in what way it is that in these individuals the blood of afflicted, persecutor, and accused, together, accommodates itself. One would look for the birth of strong characteristics here, possibly for terrible developments, out of the opposition of such material; but nothing notable ever happens in the tranquil town, and not a ripple of distinction breaks its history since those first dreadful days, unless we recall the vanished figure of Hawthorne walking all his life long in the shadow of that old witch-prosecuting ancestor, the Magistrate. But much inheritance of a thing dies with the memory of it, and when the scales dropped from the eyes of the persecutors of 1692, and they saw themselves the shedders of innocent blood, they destroyed all records that could be found, reseated the church so that relatives of the murderer and of the murdered sang their hymns side by side from the same book, and since those who had borne the stain of the scaffold in their family were not likely to make it subject of conversation, those who inflicted that stain were glad to let it be forgotten ; and it came to pass that, when the historian sought for it, he found less tradition existing relative to the occurrences of that dark and bloody period than of times of quadruple the antiquity. It reached him, though, from all unimagined avenues, from church-records, from registries of wills and deeds, from family papers, and we now have it in sufficient completeness to make us detest, if not the people, at least the influences that made the people actors in that tragedy.

Like most things of magnitude, the Salem Witchcraft had its beginnings in small things—in so small a thing, indeed, as a circle of young girls meeting together, on winter evenings, at each other's houses, to practice palmistry and such sleight-of-hand as parlor-magic had then attained. Perhaps it was as remarkable a thing as any in the whole occurrences that such meetings were countenanced at all in that place of the Puritan, and more remarkable still, that no connection was suspected between these meetings and the subsequent antics. These young girls were ten in number ; three of them were servants, and two of these are believed to have acted from malicious motives against the families where they were employed, one of them afterward admitting that she did so ; and Mary Warren's guilt, as capital witness securing the execution of seven innocent persons, being—unless we accept the hypothesis of spiritualism—as evident as it is black and damning. In addition to these there were the negro-slaves of Mr. Parris, the minister, in whose household all the first disturbances made their appearance, Tituba and her husband.

It is worthy of remark, as the historian urges, that Elizabeth Parris—a child of only nine years, but of extraordinary precocity, the daughter of the minister, himself the foremost fomenter and agitator of the troubles—was early removed by him from the scene, and placed under shelter at safe distance. Of the remainder, the most prominent were Abigail Williams, aged eleven, a niece of the minister's, and resident in his family ; Ann Putnam, aged twelve ; Betty Hubbard and Mary Walcot, both aged seventeen ; and Mercy Lewis, of the same age, a servant in the family of Ann Putnam's mother, Mrs. Ann Putnam, aged thirty, who afterward became as prominent as any in the matter of afflictions. There were a Mrs. Pope and a Mrs. Bibber, who joined the circle ; but the one was only hysterical, and the latter was detected in a trick, and their connection with the phenomena was brief. It is not unreasonable to suppose that Tituba was at the root of the whole business. Brought by Mr. Parris, who had formerly been a merchant, from the West Indies, and still but half-civilized, she was full of her wild Obeah superstitions and incantations, in which she had without doubt interested the two children in her master's family, Elizabeth Parris and Abigail Williams. Probably they invited Ann Putnam, a child of nearly the same age as themselves, to witness what they found so entertaining ; and she, confiding in her mother's servant, Mercy Lewis, an ignorant girl of seventeen, Mercy in turn interested her own companions in the matter. Sitting over the winter fires, after growing tired of their exercises in magic, it is likely that they rehearsed to each other all the marvelous tales of the primeval settlements, stories full of sheeted ghosts, with wild hints of the Indian goblin Hobbomocko, till they shuddered and laughed at the shuddering, and their terrified imaginations and excited nerves were ready for something beyond. Perfecting themselves in all they could discover of legerdemain, taught by Tituba the secret of a species of voluntary cataleptic fit, and improving on her teachings by means of their own superior intelligence, before the winter was over they had become adepts in their arts, and were ready for exhibition. It is likely that at first their object was merely to display their skill, to amuse amusement and arouse wonder, and, possibly, admiration, in their beholders, who singularly failed to perceive that it was a concerted thing among them. Perhaps, too, they were somewhat emulous of the fame of the Goodwin children, whose exploits had lately been on every tongue. When the crowds, who afterward flocked to see those whom ministers and doctors had pronounced bewitched, witnessed their appalling condition, they were overwhelmed with horror ; for, "whatever opinion may be formed," says Mr. Upham, "of the moral or mental condition of the afflicted children, as to their sanity and responsibility, there can be no doubt that they were great actors. In mere jugglery and sleight-of-hand, they bear no mean comparison with the workers of wonders, in that line, of our own day. Long practice had given them complete control over their countenances, intonations of voice, and the entire muscular and nervous organization of their bodies ; so that they could at will, and on the instant, go into fits and convulsions ; swoon and fall to the floor ; put their frames into strange contortions ; bring the blood to the face and send it back again. They could be deadly pale at one moment, at the next flushed ; their hands would be clinched and held together as with a vice ; their limbs stiff and rigid or wholly relaxed ; their teeth would be set, they would go through the paroxysms of choking and strangulation, and gasp for breath, bringing froth and blood from the mouth ; they would utter all sorts of screams in unearthly tones ; their eyes remain fixed, sometimes bereft of all light and expression,

"THE REV. GEORGE BURROUGHS WAS ACCUSED OF WITCHCRAFT ON THE EVIDENCE OF FEATS OF STRENGTH, TRIED, HUNG, AND BURIED BENEATH THE GALLOWS."

cold and stony, and sometimes kindled into flames of passion; they would pass into the state of somnambulism, without aim or conscious direction in their movements, looking at some point where was no apparent object of vision, with a wild, unmeaning glare. There are some indications that they had acquired the art of ventriloquism; or they so wrought upon the imaginations of the beholders that the sounds of the motions and voices of invisible beings were believed to be heard. They would start, tremble, and be pallid before apparitions seen, of course, only by themselves; but their acting was so perfect that all present thought they saw them, too. They would address and hold colloquy with spectres and ghosts, and the responses of the unseen beings would be audible to the fancy of the bewildered crowd. They would follow with their eyes the airy visions so that others imagined they also beheld them."

Mr. Upham calls this a high dramatic achievement; but he goes on to state that the Attorney-General, a barrister fresh from the Inns of Court at London, was often present, together with many others who had seen the world, and were competent to detect trickery; and it is, after all, difficult to believe that this parcel of rude girls could have acquired so much dexterity, and that no diseased condition of mind and nerve assisted them, and that the fits, which were at first voluntary, did not at last take control of them and all their powers. Notwithstanding this doubt, it is plain that their magic came in on such occasions as the pin-pricking ; as, for instance, when one of them, not wishing to reply, had a pin apparently run through both her upper and lower lip, and no wound or festering following. On such occasions, too, as that when they were found with their arms tied, and hung upon a hook, or their wrists bound fast with a cord, after the manner of the Davenport Brothers of to-day ; as that, when an iron spindle, missing for some time from a house in the village, was suddenly snatched out of the air from the hand of an apparition ; or that, when one of them being afflicted by a spectre in a white sheet, invisible to other than herself, caught and tore the corner of the sheet, and showed the real cloth in her hand to the spectators, who received it undoubtingly. Their catalepsy, though, or whatever it may be called, was of use to them throughout — whether they chewed soap till they foamed at the mouth, and expertly twisted their supple bodies into long-practiced contortions, or whether what was feigned at first grew real afterward, and they were seized by the flame they had kindled, and became demented by the contagious delirium. It is well understood that the Shakers of the present day are capable of producing similar conditions—fits, distortions, trances in which visions are imagined to be seen ; and something of the same sort is frequent in the camp-meeting revivals, while shrieking hysterics are now known to be as voluntary as winking ; and it has even been discovered that fixing the eyes and the attention upon a bright spot at a short distance away will induce a state of coma. Whether they had learned the possibility of such things, or merely simulated them, it is almost impossible to believe that these girls, in the depth of depravity to which they descended, were not victims of a temporary insanity. Their ready wit and make-shift would lend a color to this supposition, as being only the cunning of the insane, if there had not been so much method in their madness, and there were not too much evidence of a directing hand behind them.

Mr. Upham thinks that they became intoxicated with the terrible success of their imposture, and having sowed the wind, were swept away by the whirlwind ; they appeared, he says, as the prosecutors of every poor creature that was tried, to such degree that their wickedness seems to transcend the capabilities of human crime ; but he goes on to remark that "there is, perhaps, a slumbering element in the heart of man that sleeps forever in the bosom of the innocent and good, and requires the perpetration of a great sin to wake it into action ; but which, when once aroused, impels the transgressor onward with increasing momentum, as the descending ball is accelerated in its course. It may be that crime begets an appetite for crime, which, like all other appetites, is not quieted, but inflamed by gratification."

A large part of the difficulty in determining the truth about these girls may vanish if we recall the declaration of the British judge, a few years since, upon the case of Constance Kent, confessing the murder of her little half-brother, where he remarked it to be a fact that there was a point in the existence of the young, when,

just coming to the full sense of life, and occupied with that, and generally with a nervous system so delicately organized as easily to be thrown out of balance, they seem to be destitute of all natural feeling, of all moral perception, and pliant to any wickedness. These young girls of Salem Village, some of greater precocity than others, were probably all of them within the scope of this declaration, and at an age when they needed careful shielding and observation, instead of being left, as they were, to the companionship of servants—servants whose duller minds and lower breeding reduced all difference of age to nothing ; and the written and signed confession of their ringleader still remains to render one very cautious in assigning the explanation of their misdeeds to any preternatural or even abnormal cause. It is known, at any rate, that they were several times discovered in deception ; once, on being reproved for it, they boldly answered that they must have a little sport ; on another time, one of them was plainly seen to be practising a trick with pins ; and, again, one of them crying out that she was being stabbed with a knife, a broken piece of a knife was found upon her, but a young man in the audience immediately declared that, on the day before, he had broken his knife, this afflicted person being present, and thrown the broken part away, and he produced the haft and remaining portion of the blade to prove it, and though the girl was reprimanded, she was used, just the same, for witness in other cases.

The state of feeling in the Colonies and elsewhere could not have been more propitious to their undertaking than it was at the time when they opened their drama. Cotton Mather, whose mind was a seething caldron of superstitions, had just published the account of the afflicted Goodwin children ; Goody Morse was living in her own house at Newbury, under sentence of death, sentence pronounced in Boston, it having been found impossible hitherto to convict a person for witchcraft in Essex County ; and Margaret Jones, and Mistress Anne Hibbins, a sister of Governor Bellingham and one of the figures of the "Scarlet Letter," had, not long before, been hung for practising the black art ; they were the free-thinkers of that day who doubted the verity of witchcraft— Addison believed in it, Edmund Fairfax, the translator of Tasso, believed in it, Sir Thomas Browne gave in court his testimony in behalf of its reality ; Blackstone, the fountain of law, asserted that to deny the existence of witchcraft was to contradict the word of God ; King James had written diatribes on witches and had persecuted them ; Queen Elizabeth had persecuted them ; William Penn had presided at the trial of two women for witchcraft ; thirty years after the executions in Salem, Dr. Watts expressed his persuasion that there was much agency of the devil and some real witches in that affair ; and so deeply rooted and long in dying was the superstition, that in 1766 a Presbyterian synod in Scotland denounced, as a national sin, the repeal of the penal laws against witchcraft ; in 1808 women were abused for witches by a whole population within sixty miles of London, and so lately as the beginning of this century Father Altizzo was imprisoned at Rome for sorcery, and there were prosecutions for witchcraft in some of the interior districts of our own Southern States. In the midst of such universal darkness, the people of Salem were not behind the spirit of their age when fancying that their village had become the battle-ground of Antichrist; and possibly they recovered sooner from their delusion than other communities of less sturdy and self-asserting habits of thought might have done. The village, too, presented an excellent field of operation, for it had for many years been torn with dissensions; there had been violent jealousies, wrangles and lawsuits over the acquisition of large property, through industry and enterprise, by people once in less prosperous circumstances, as for example, the Nurses, and quarrels with the "Topsfield Men," connections of the Nurses, in relation to boundaries, resulting in fisticuff encounters and lasting enmities. There had, moreover, been trouble in the parish in relation to the impossibility of procuring a minister who should please all parties, Mr. Bayley, Mr. Burroughs and Mr. Deodat Lawson having been obliged to leave, owing to the hostilities, and Mr. Sam. Parris being settled in their place. Mr. Parris, among several singular qualities, seems to have been almost destitute of sympathy—he once told some men whose mo'her's execution he had been instrumental in procuring, that while they thought her innocent and he thought her guilty, the matter between them was merely a difference of opinion; he was possessed of great talent, and of an inordinate ambition; passionately fond of power, and constantly stirring up scenes that might lead to it, during the whole time of his career he kept the parish in a broil; he had at last grown so unpopular, that some bold stroke became necessary in order to regain lost ground, and when the children in his family commenced their performances, it is thought that he saw his advantage, and used it, to the pulling down of those who opposed him, and the setting-up of the standard of the Church, in his person, over all other authority. Probably, as Cotton Mather did, he aspired to be the chief champion of Christianity, and therefore the more exceedingly he could inflame the people, and then the more effectually quench the flame, the greater glory must redound to him and his ministry; and it is possible that neither he nor the "afflicted children" had originally any idea of the lengths to which the thing would go; but once committed, there was no retreat.

When now the girls began to exhibit their new accomplishments at home, their frightened parents gave them medicine; of course this did not modify their symptoms, and presently the physician was summoned. Finding that none of his appliances changed their condition, Dr. Griggs took refuge in a common saying of the time, which had sheltered the ignorance of many another doctor, and declared that an evil hand had been laid upon them. Then Mr. Parris scented his prey in an instant; he kept the children in an agitation, noised the affair abroad till it became the talk of town and countryside, and the neighbors ran to see the convulsions of the afflicted, shivered with awe when the Sabbath meetings were disturbed by their outbursts, believed they saw the yellowbird that Ann Putnam saw "sitting on the minister's hat as it hangs on the pin in the pulpit;" the families of the various afflicted ones fasted and prayed, and finally Mr. Parris called a convocation of the ministers to witness the proceedings of these crazy children, half diseased,

half evil. Upon this the children brought out all the scenes in their repertory at once, and the ministers were astounded; always ready for combats with Satan, here they had him on open ground; they appointed a day of exhortation over the afflicted, and increased the excitement of the people to fury, so that nothing was thought of but the sufferings of these victims of the wrath of the Evil One, sufferings whose reality no one disbelieved; all business became suspended, all labor was left, and the whole community was in a frenzy of fanaticism. A few individuals did n t join the outcry: Martha Corey did not believe there were any witches—presently she was accused for one and hung; the Nurses and Cloyses and Joseph Putnam objected to the minister's allowing the children of his family to disturb the meeting without so much as a rebuke, and withdrew from their attendance at the church—Rebecca Nurse was hung, Sarah Cloyse was imprisoned, and Joseph Putnam escaped only by arming every member of his family and keeping a horse under saddle night and day for six months, determined, if the marshal came for him with a small posse, to resist, but if with an overwhelming force, to fly, choosing rather the mercies of the savage heathen of the forest than the barbarities of these frantic Chri tians.

It is a common error to suppose that the three learned professions lead the people in point of intelligence. On the contrary, trained in grooves not easy to leave, they remain as they were in the beginning, and almost all advance comes from the outside. This was never better exemplified than in the Witchcraft delusion. If the physicians then had possessed either acuteness, skill, or candor, they would have checked the girls in their first spasms; if the ministers had been what they should have been ere daring to undertake the cure of souls, instead of lending countenance to their pretensions and praying over the girls, they would have punished them and made them fear the consequences of their manœuvres; if the lawyers had exercised any quality which a lawyer should possess, they would have sifted their testimony till it blew away in the wind, and would have utterly cast out the evidence of spectres, instead of greedily receiving it and hounding on the poor wretches to their death. When justices, deacons, doctors and gentry hurried to wonder over and sympathize with the young impostors, when their leaders came to be mad, it is no marvel that the people lost their head and followed after. In the faith that the girls were bewitched, and that Satan acted only through human agencies, they clamored to know who it was that had bewitched them; and thus beset, the girls, either at random or because there was no one to befriend her, or at Mr. Parris's half-hinted suggestion, timidly pronounced a name. "Good," they said, " Good"—cheating their conscience, perhaps, by making it only a surname; they had no such timidity by-and-by; and Sarah Good was consequently apprehended. When she was examined, two others had been named, arrested, and were examined with her.

Sarah Good was a poor creature—homeless, destitute, deserted by her husband, with a family of children to support by odds and ends of work, by begging from door to door, and scraping together in any way what little she could. Doubtless she was a nuisance in the neighborhood, as most impecunious and shiftless people are, and her reputation was not satisfactory. Her fate was certain from the onset. The people—who were full of horror and of pity for the tortured girls; who had been told by the physicians that they were bewitched; who had seen the ministers oracularly confirm this statement; who had heard Mr. Parris make it the subject of his vehement discourses Sunday after Sunday, while the distemper of the girls alarmed the congregation; who had lately done nothing but look for the guilty author of this diabolism, drew a breath of relief when at last the witch was named; so plausible a person. A vagrant and friendless; and it must be admitted that Sarah Good and Mrs. Osburne—an elderly person, sometimes bedridden, sometimes distracted, who absented herself from meeting—and the slave Tituba, were the best possible selections that the cunning hussies could have made; and the people were satisfied. Mrs. Osburne died in prison nine months afterward; Tituba confessed—as she subsequently averred, under stress of beatings from Mr. Parris—and, lying in jail a year and a month, was finally sold for her fees; but Sarah Good drank her cup, bitter all her life long, to the bitter dregs. The meeting-house was thronged at her examination; she was placed on a platform in full sight of all there; Mr. Parris had excited every one with his impassioned opening prayer; the array of magistrates, marshal and constable were enough to strike awe into her soul at any time, much more when her life was at stake. Acquainted with want, with sorrow and obloquy, her heart had been hardened, and she gave back no mild answers to the catechising. The justices assumed her guilt to be already established, endeavored to make her involve herself, gave leading questions to the witnesses, allowed all manner of abominable interruptions, and browbeat and abused her. When the afflicted children were introduced, at a glance of her eye they straightway fainted and went into spasms, cried out that they were pinched and pricked and throttled, and fell stiff as the dead. Upon being taken to her and touched by her, the color returned to their faces, their limbs relaxed, they immediately became calm and well; so that it seemed to be demonstrated before the eyes of the credulous audience that the malign miasm had been received back again into the witch.

She herself could not tell what to make of it, and never doubted the fact that the girls suffered as they seemed to do; she only declared that it was not she that caused it, and must be the others—which simple exclamation the justices used as a confession of her own guilt, and accusation and evidence against the others. "What is it that you say," asked Hathorne, "when you go muttering away from persons' houses?" "If I must tell, I will tell," she answers. "Do tell us, then," he urges. "If I must tell, I will tell: it is the Commandments. I may say my Commandments, I hope." "What Commandment is it?" Poor Sarah Good could not for the life of her remember a Commandment. "If I must tell you, I will tell," she says then—"it is a psalm;" and after a time she murmurs some fragment that she has succeeded in recalling. Before long her husband was brought in to testify against her. She was sent to prison—thrice leaping off her horse, railing against the magistrates, and essaying to take her own life—and afterward loaded down with iron fetters and with cords, since it was supposed a witch needed double fastenings, till led out, our months later, to her execution. Meanwhile her child, five years old, was apprehended for a witch; the marks of her little teeth were shown on Ann Putnam's arm; Mercy Lewis and the others produced pins with which she had pricked them; she was committed to prison and loaded with chains like her mother. Outraged, oppressed, and feeling there was no justice in the world unless the Powers that rule it made her word true, when, upon the scaffold, the cruel minister, Nicholas Noyes, told Sarah Good she was a witch, and she knew she was a witch, she turned upon him and cried, "You are a liar! and God shall give you blood to drink!" Twenty-five years afterward, and unrepenting, Nicholas Noyes died of an internal hemorrhage, the vital torrent pouring from his mouth and strangling him with his own blood.

After the first three witches had been proclaimed, the business began in earnest, and the girls "cried out upon" enough to keep the magistrates' hands full; consternation and terror ran like wildfire through the community, which was unlettered and ignorant to a large degree, the learning of the fathers having died with them, and the schools not being yet established; presently everybody was either accused or accusing, there was a witch in every house, the only safety for any was in suspecting a neighbor. If one expressed doubt of the afflicted children, he was marked from that moment. The Rev. Francis Dane suspected them; his family were cried out upon, two of his children and many of his grandchildren being imprisoned, and some sentenced to death. The Rev. John Higginson —of whom it was said, "his very presence puts vice out of countenance, his conversation is a glimpse of heaven"—disbelieved in them; his daughter Anna was committed as a witch. Husbands were made to criminate their wives, children, their parents; when one of the accusing girls fell away, she was herself accused, but knowing what to do, was saved by a confession of impossibilities. Anything was taken for evidence, the nightmares of this one, the drunken fantasies of that, the hysterics of the other, and any careless gossip that never should have been uttered at all. If a prisoner dared use any self-vindication, the vanity and anger of the magistrates were kindled against that one in especial. Hundreds were under arrest; hundreds confessed to what they never did, as the only means to save their lives, though afterward frequently retracting their confessions and going cheerfully to death; the prisons were full, and executions began. The accusations of the afflicted girls mounted by degrees from simple witchcraft and writing in the Black Man's book, with the familiar of a yellow-bird suckling the fingers, to that of a baptism and sacrament of blood administered by the devil himself, and finally to that of fell and terrible murders. Their narratives were all of the same character, their imaginations filthy and limited in flight, and the only assertions in the whole of their rodomontade of any brilliance was Tituba's reply as to how they went to their place of meeting. "We ride upon sticks, and are there presently," and the description of Mr. Burroughs trumpet's tone to convene his witches—"a sound that reached over the country far and wide, sending its blasts to Andover, and wakening its echoes along the Merrimack to Cape Ann and the uttermost settlements everywhere." Kindness had no effect upon the girls; when Mrs. Procter—three of whose children their representations had cast into prison, and whom they had torn away from her home, leaving her forlorn "little maid" of four years old to come out and scan the passers-by, in hopes each one might be her father or her mother, her brother or her sister come back—when Mrs. Procter mildly said to one of them, "Dear child, it is not so," and solemnly added. "There is another judgment, dear child," they redoubled their convulsions, and grew so outrageous that John Procter, protecting his wife from their insults, was himself accused and hung. The prisoners, meanwhile, were crowded in such noisome dungeons, that many died and many lost their reason; some also were tortured to procure confession—feet and head bound together till the blood poured from eyes and nose.

The accusations were by no means confined to Salem; Andover, Beverly, Boston, were ransacked to fill them—the girls had tasted blood and were pitiless. A Mrs. Easty was taken from the old Crowninshield Farm in Topsfield (now owned by Mr. Thomas W. Pierce, and brought to court; she was a woman of station and character; even the magistrates were affected by her mien; and though Ann Putnam and others cried, "Oh, Goody Easty, Goody Easty, you are the woman, you are the woman!" she was discharged, having endured several weeks' confinement; but upon that there arose such an uproar among the girls, such fresh fits and tormentings, that, after having enjoyed her home for only two days, she was again arrested by the brutal Marshal Herrick, and presently hung. But even in her last hour this noble woman sent to the Governor a petition in behalf of her fellow-prisoners, yet asking no favor for herself. Mr. Upham describes a scene at the trial of Sarah Cloyse, taken every incident from the record, which perfectly illustrates the callousness of these girls.

"Then Sarah Cloyse asked for water, and sat down, as one seized with a dying fainting-fit; and several of the afflicted fell into fits, and some of them cried out, 'Oh, her spirit has gone to prison to her sister Nurse!'

"The audacious lying of the witnesses; the horrid monstrousness of their charges against Sarah Cloyse, of having bitten the flesh of the Indian brute, and drank herself and distributed to others as deacon, at an infernal sacrament, the blood of the wicked creatures making these foul and devilish declarations, known by her to be utterly and wickedly false; and the fact that they were believed by the deputy, the council, and the assembly, were more than she could bear. Her soul sickened at such unimaginable depravity and wrong; her nervous system gave way; she fainted and sank to the floor. The manner in which the girls turned the incident against her shows how they were hardened to all human feeling, and the cunning art which, on all occasions, characterized their proceedings. That such an insolent interruption and disturbance, on their part, was permitted without rebuke from the Court, is a perpetual dishonor to every member of it. The scene exhibited at this moment, in the meeting-house, is worthy of an attempt to imagine. The most terrible sensation was naturally produced by the swooning of the prisoner, the loudly uttered and savage mockery of the girls, and their going simultaneously into fits, screaming at the top of their voices, twisting into all possible attitudes. stiffened as in death, or gasping with convulsive spasms of agony, and crying out. at intervals, 'There is the Black Man whispering in Cloyse's ear.' 'There is a yellow-bird flying round her head.' John Indian, on such occasions, used to confine his achievements to tumbling and rolling his ugly body about the floor. The deepest commiseration was felt by all for the 'afflicted,' and men and women rushed to hold and soothe them. There was, no doubt, much loud screeching, and some miscellaneous faintings through the whole crowd. At length, by bringing the sufferers into contact with Goody Cloyse, the diabolical fluid passed back into her, they were all relieved, and the examination was resumed."

In fact, neither age nor condition had any effect upon the prosecutors. Rebecca Jacobs, partially deranged, was snatched from her four young children, one of them an infant, and the others who were able to walk following after her. crying bitterly. Martha Carrier, who the children said had promise from the Black Man of b ing Queen of Hell, and who had sternly rebuked the magistrates, and declared she had seen no man so black as themselves, was made to hear her children, seven or eight years old, confess themselves witches who had set their hands to the book, testify against her, and procure her death. Rebecca Nurse, past three score and ten, wife of a wealthy citizen, venerated by high and low, was brought to trial in her infirm condition, accused by the girls at the very time when she was praying for them. On the jury's bringing in a verdict of innocence, they were reprimanded by the Chief-Justice, and remanded to confinement till they brought in a verdict of guilty; and though her neighbors made affidavits and petitions in her behalf, she was condemned; after which Mr. Parris, who had long since gotten affairs into his own hands, had intimidated outsiders, and was having everything his own way, prepared one of his most solemn scenes to further excite the people; and Mrs. Nurse, delicate, if not dying as it was. after her shameful trial, her cruel and indecent exposures, was brought into church, covered with chains, and there excommunicated by her old pastor, Nicholas Noyes—the crowd of spectators believing they saw a woman not only lost for this life, but barred out from salvation in the life to come. She was thrown, after death, into a hole beneath the gallows; but her husband and sons recovered her body in the night, brought it home to her weeping daughters, and buried it in her own garden.

With that, the girls, grown bold, had flown at higher game than any, the Rev. George Burroughs, one of Mr. Parris's rivals and predecessors. This person had suffered almost everything in Salem ere leaving it for Casco Bay; he had lost his wife and children there, his salary had not been paid him, and he had even been arrested in his pulpit for the debt of his wife's funeral expenses, which he had previously paid by an order on the church-treasurer. The malignities that he now endured are only explicable by remembering his unpopularity in Salem; he was cast into a black dungeon, accused of witchcraft on the evidence of such feats of strength as holding out a gun by inserting the joint of a finger in the muzzle, and after that accused of the murder of his two wives and of his children, of Mr. Lawson's wife and child, and of various others, covered with all abuses, and finally hung, and buried beneath the gallows, with his chin and foot protruding from the ground. Mr. Upham gives a chapter in his trial too graphically to escape quotation here:

"The examination of Mr. Burroughs presented a spectacle, all things considered, of rare interest and curiosity: the grave dignity of the magistrates; the plain, dark figure of the prisoner; the half-crazed, half-demoniac aspect of the girls; the wild, excited crowd; the horror, rage, and pallid exasperation of Lawson, Goodman Fuller, and others, also of the relatives and friends of Burroughs's two former wives, as the deep damnation of their taking off and the secrets of their bloody graves were being brought to light; and the child on the stand telling her awful tales of ghosts in winding-sheets, with napkins round their heads, pointing to their death-wounds, and saying that 'their blood did cry for vengeance' upon their murderer. The prisoner stands alone: all were raving around him, while he is amazed, astounded at such folly and wrong in others, and humbly sensible of his own unworthiness, bowed down under the mysterious Providence that permitted such things for a season, yet strong and steadfast in conscious innocence and uprightness."

But though such countless arrests and trials and condemnations were had, and so many executions, the most startling incident among them all was the death of old Giles Corey.

Giles Corey was a man of marked traits, not the least marked of which was an unbending will and a heart that knew no fear. In the course of his long life he had never submitted to a wrong without retaliation, he had suffered no encroachments on his rights, he had cared nothing for the speech of other people, but had always spoken his own mind, let who would stand at the door; he had quarrelled with his acquaintances, beaten his servants, sued his neighbors for slander, and, such experience tending toward small self-control, he had been involved in ceaseless litigation, and as often as not had been in the right. Late in life he married, for his third wife, Martha, a woman of intelligence beyond her time, and joined the Church; and he was eighty years old when the Witchcraft excitement began. With his ardent and eager temperament, nothing abated by age, he was immediately interested in the afflicted children, and soon as fanatical as the worst in regard to them. That his wife should laugh at it all, should suppose those God-fearing men, the magistrates, blind, should assert there was no such thing as a witch at all, and, when he had seen their agonies with his own eyes, that the afflicted children did but dissemble, and should hide his saddle that he might stay at home, and no longer swell the press that urged the matter on, filled him with amazement and rage; he exclaimed angrily that the devil was in her, and, for all he knew, she might be a witch herself! When his wife was arrested, these words of his were remembered; he was piled in court with artful questions, whose replies must needs be unfavorable to her; two of his sons-in-law testified to his recent disagreement with her, to his bewitched cattle, and other troubles, and he was obliged to give a deposition against her. But he could not be forced to make the deposition amount to anything; and, indignant with him for that contumacy, his wife's accusers became his own, and he was cast into jail for a wizard. Once imprisoned, with leisure to reflect, conscious that he had never used witchcraft in his life, he began to believe that others might be as innocent as he, to be aware of the hallucination to which he had been subject, to see that his wife, by that time sentenced to execution, was a guiltless martyr, to feel his old love and tenderness for her return upon him, to be filled with remorse for his anger with her, for his testimony and deposition, and with his old hot wrath against his two sons-in-laws, whose word had done her to death.

He comprehended the whole situation, that unless he confessed to a lie nothing could save him, that if he were tried he would certainly be condemned, and his property would be confiscated under the attainder. He desired in his extremity some punishment on his two unfaithful sons-in-law, some reward for his two faithful ones. He sent for the necessary instruments and made his will, giving all his large property to his two faithful sons-in-law, and guarding the gift with every careful form of words known to the law. That properly done and witnessed, his resolve was taken. He determined never to be tried. If he was not tried, he could not be condemned; if he was not condemned, this disposition of his property could not be altered. The only way to accomplish this was by refusing to plead either guilty or not guilty. And this he did. When taken into court he maintained a stubborn silence, he refused to open his lips; and till the prisoner answered "guilty" or "not guilty," the trial could not take place. For this, also, there was but one remedy, and old Giles Corey knew it; but his mind was made up; it was the least atonement he could make his wife—to requite the sons that had been loyal to her, and to meet himself a harder fate than he had given her. Perhaps, too, he saw that it needed such a thing to awaken the people, and he was the voluntary sacrifice. He received unflinchingly the sentence of the *Peine forte et dure*, and from that moment never uttered a syllable. This unspeakably dreadful torture condemned one to a dark cell, there, with only a strip of clothing, to be laid upon the floor with an iron weight upon the chest, receiving the alternate fare of three mouthfuls of bread on one day, and on the next three draughts of the nearest stagnant water, till obstinacy yielded or death arrived. In Giles Corey's case—excommunication having been previously pronounced on a self-murderer by the inexorable church-members—the punishment was administered in the outside air, and the weights were of stone; he was strong, in spite of years; the anguish was long; pressed by the burden, his tongue protruded from his mouth, a constable struck it back with his staff, but not a word came with it, and he died unflinching, never pleading either guilty or not guilty. With this before unheard-of judicial murder in the Colonies, a universal horror shuddered through the people already surfeited with horrors, and all at once their eyes opened to the enormity of these proceedings. Three days afterward, the last procession of victims, once hooted and insulted as they went, jolted now in silence through the long and tedious ways to the summit of Witch Hill, and, taking their farewell look at the wide panorama of land and sea, the last witches were hanged. It was in vain for Cotton Mather to utter his incendiary eloquence beneath the gallows and endeavor to rekindle the dying fires in the breasts of the sorry and silent people; for Mr. Noyes to exclaim, as the bodies swung off, "What a sad thing it is to see eight firebrands of hell hanging there!" The ministers exhorted, the frantic girls cried out on one and another, and flew at so high a quarry as the wife of the Rev. John Hale, a woman of almost perfect life; and though Mrs. Hale's husband had persecuted others, when the thunderbolt fell on his own roof, he awoke to his delirium: then the Commoners of Andover instituted suits for slander, and with that the bubble burst, and not another witch was hung. The whole Colony was shaken with remorse, and the reaction from the excitement was like death. The accusing girls came out of their convulsions unregarded; one or two afterward married; the rest, with the exception of Ann Putnam, led openly shameless lives. Seven years afterward, bereft of her father and mother, and with the care of a large family of young brothers and sisters, and a constitution utterly broken down by her career of fits and contortions, Ann Putnam read in the open church a confession of her crimes, partook of the communion, and the tenth year following she died. It is a brief and very strange confession; in it all the sin is laid upon Satan, and so artlessly that one can but give her innocence the benefit of a doubt; and whether the girl was the subject of delusive trances or of wickedness, must remain a mystery until the science of psychology has made further advances than it has done to-day. When the people had fully come to their senses, the jury that had passed verdict on the accused wrote and circulated an avowal of their regret; Judge Sewall rose in his place in the Old South Church in Boston and made a public acknowledgment of his error, and supplication for forgiveness, and every year thereafter kept a day of humiliation and prayer; but Chief-Justice Stoughton remained as infatuated at the last as at the first; and of the ministers who had been active in the vile work, Cotton Mather, Sam. Parris, Nicholas Noyes, there is not a particle of evidence that one of them repented or regretted it. But Salem Village was ruined, its farms were neglected, its roads broken up, its fences scattered, its buildings out of order, industrial pursuits were destroyed, famine came, taxes were due and lands were sold to meet them, whole families moved away, and the place became almost depopulated. One spot there, says the historian, bears marks of the blight to-day—the old meeting-house road.' "The Surveyor of Highways ignores it. The old, gray, moss-covered stone walls are dilapidated and thrown out of line. Not a house is on either of its borders, and no gate opens or path leads to any. Neglect and desertion brood over the contiguous ground. On both sides there are the remains of cellars, which declare that once it was lined by a considerable population. Along this road crowds thronged in 1692, for weeks and months, to witness the examinations."

It is a satisfaction to the vindictive reader of the annals of this time to know that Sam. Parris —guilty of divination by his own judgment, since he had plainly used the afflicted children for that purpose—was dismissed from his pastorate, where he had played the part rather of wolf than of shepherd, and finished his days in ignominy and want. While every reader will be glad to know that a good man, Joseph Green, came to soothe the sorrows and bind up the wounds, and destroy as much as might be all memory of wrong and suffering in the place. But though, for a few years, various Legislatures passed small acts of acknowledgment and compensation, yet, wars and other troubles supervening, and possible shame at reopening the past, it so happens that for several of the murdered people the attainder has never been taken off to the present day.

NEWBURYPORT.

Leaving Salem behind, the traveler passes beautiful Beverly, the home of Lucy Larcom, and whose beach is neighbor of the wonderful singing one where the sands make mystical music under foot, passes the little town which Gail Hamilton renders interesting by living there, passes Ipswich, the old Agawam, the picture of an English village, in a dimple between hills, and with the tides of its quiet river curving about it, passes ancient Rowley, and arrives at another historic and famous town, whose rulers once changed its name to Portland, but whose people scorned to do so much as even to refuse the new name, but continued to the present day to call it Newburyport.

Newburyport is in some external respects not unlike the neighboring towns of note, but in others she is a place by herself. Situated on the Merrimack—the busiest river in the world, and one of the loveliest, and whose banks, owing to the configuration of the coast, seem here, like the Nile banks, to run out and push back the sea that it may have the greater room to expand its beauty in—the town has both a scenic and a social isolation which has had a great deal to do with the characteristics of its population. These characteristics, with but one or two exceptions, have been the same for all time, since time began for Newburyport. It is true that the municipality, which once petitioned General Court to relieve it of the burden of the old wandering negress Juniper, has so far improved as now to be giving a pauper outside the almshouse an allowance out of which he has built him a cottage in an adjoining town, and bought him some shares of railroad stock; but for the rest, the place has known no change; it has not varied from its dullness since the Embargo laid a heavy hand upon it and the Great Fire scattered ashes over it, and the people mind their own business to-day just as thoroughly as they did when they pronounced the verdict upon the body of Elizabeth Hunt in 1693, "We judge, according to our best light and contents, that the death of said Elizabeth Hunt was * * * by some soden stoping of her breath." Strangers come into town, stay a while, and depart, leaving behind them some trail of romance or of misbehavior—the citizen takes small heed of them, and presently forgets them; so rarely do they assimilate themselves with the population, that the names there to-day are the names to be found in the chronicles of 1635, and, unmixed with strange blood, generations hand down a name till it comes to stand for a trait. The people, too, have a singular intelligence for a community not metropolitan, possibly because, being a seafaring tribe, their intercourse with foreign countries enlightens them to an unusual degree. The town, except for one religious revival that lasted forty days, suspended business, drew up the shipping in the dock, and absorbed master and mistress, man and maid, has seldom been disturbed by any undue contagion of popular feeling, has seldom followed a fashion in politics unsuggested by its own necessities, and has been in fact as sufficient to itself as the dew of Eden. The dissimilarity of its population from that of other places is only illustrated by the story of a sailor, impressed into the British Navy too hurriedly to get the address of a friend, and who, after tossing about the world for fifty years, returned home and advertised for "an old shipmate whom he desired to share a fortune with." Neither has the town ever been a respecter of persons, but, democratic in the true acceptation of the term, wealth is but little accounted where almost every one is comfortable, talent gives no more pre-eminence than can be grasped by means of it, and it if were the law now, as it was then, five leading citizens would just as easily be arrested and fined for being absent from town-meeting at eight o'clock in the morning as they were in 1638. United to all this there is an extremely independent way of thinking hereditary among the people. In 1640 Thomas Scott paid a fine of ten shillings rather than learn the catechism, and was allowed to do so; a century later, Richard Bartlet refused communion with a church whose pastor wore a wig, asserting with assurance that all who wore wigs, unless repenting before death, would certainly be damned; not long before, the Rev. John Tufts here struck a death-blow at Puritanism by issuing a book of twenty-seven psalm-tunes to be sung in public worship, five tunes only having previously been used; an act so stoutly contested as an inroad of the Scarlet Woman—for, said his opponents, it is first singing by rule, then praying by rule, and then popery—that it was probably owing to the persecutions of the long warfare that subsequently the innovator left his parish in dudgeon under a charge of indecent behavior; and though none of the churches reached the point attained by one some dozen miles away, which voted, "This meeting, not having unity with John Collins's testimony, desires him to be silent till the Lord speak by him to the satisfaction of the meeting," yet there stands on the record the instruction to a committee appointed to deal with certain recusants, "to see if something could not be said or done to draw them to our communion again, and *if we cannot draw them by fair means, then to determine what means to take with them.*" Some one once said that Newburyport was famous for its piety and privateering, but in these instructions the piety and privateering are oddly intermingled. This same independence of thought found notable expression when, in the early days, Boston and Salem, alarmed at the incursions of the Indians, proposed to the next settlements the building of a stone wall eight feet high to inclose them all, as a rampart against the common foe; which proposition Newburyport scouted with disdain, and declared the wall should be a living one, made of men, and forthwith built a garrison-house on her borders. And it is the same quality that afterward appeared when, some time previous to the Boston tea-party, the first act of the Revolution was signalized in Newburyport by the confiscation of a cargo of tea under direction of the town authorities: and that prompted

"STANDING ON THE QUARTER-DECK, HE SUDDENLY TURNED AND ORDERED THE BRITISH FLAG TO BE STRUCK!"

the Stamp Act Riots, and made it a fact that not a single British stamp was ever paid for or used in Newburyport; and that, during all the long and trying struggle of the Revolution, did not allow a single town-school to be suspended. The old town has no trivial history, as these circumstances might intimate. Long before the Revolution, at the popular uprising and the imprisonment of Sir Edmund Andros, old Sam Bartlet galloped off, so eager for the fray, that "his long rusty sword, trailing on the ground, left, as it came in contact with the stones in the road, a stream of fire all the way." It was Lieutenant Jacques, of Newburyport, who put an end to the war with the Norridgewock Indians, by killing their ally and inciter, the French Jesuit, Sebastian Rallé. Here Arnold's expedition against Quebec encamped and recruited; and here were built and manned not only the privateers, that the better feeling of to-day calls pirates, which raked British commerce to the value of millions into this port, but the sloop Wasp, which fought as fiercely as her namesake fights, in three months capturing thirteen merchantmen, engaging four ships-of-the-line, and finally, after a bitter struggle, going down with all her men at the guns and all her colors flying. It is still interesting to read of her exploits, copied in the journal of the old Marine Insurance rooms as the news came in day by day, and to fancy the ardor and spirit with which those lines were penned by hands long since ashes; ardor and spirit universally shared, since, before that brief career of valor, Newburyport had on the 31st of May, anticipated the Declaration of Independence, published on the 19th of July following, by instructing the Congress at Philadelphia that, if the Colonies should be declared independent, "this town will, with their lives and fortunes, support them in the measure." Here, too, was built the first ship that ever displayed our flag upon the Thames, a broom at her peak that day, after Van Tromp's fashion, to tell the story of how she had swept the seas. Nor is the town unfamiliar with such daring deeds as that done, during the Revolution, when a British transport of four guns was observed in the bay veering and tacking to and fro through the fog, as if uncertain of her whereabouts, and, surmising that she supposed herself in Boston Bay, Captain Offin Boardman, with his men, went off in a whaleboat and offered his services to pilot her in, the offer being of course accepted, the ship hove to, and Captain Offin Boardman presently standing on the quarter-deck exchanging the usual greetings with the master of the transport while his companions mounted to his side; that done, he suddenly turned and ordered the British flag to be struck, his order was executed, and, wholly overpowered in their surprise, the crew and the transport were safely carried over the bar and moored at the wharves in Newburyport. Indeed, her history declares the place to have been in other respects far in advance of many of her contemporaries; she had, not only the first of our ships upon the Thames, but the first chain-bridge in America, as well as the first toll-bridge, initiated the first insurance company, had the first incorporated woolen mill, the first incorporated academy, the first female high school, two of the first members of the Anti-Slavery Society, which numbered twelve in all, the first volunteer company for the Revolution, the first volunteer

company against the Rebellion, the first bishop, and the first graduate of Harvard—the last at a time when sundry students guilty of misdemeanors were publicly whipped by the president, a punishment, whether unfortunately or otherwise, now out of date in that institution, to which Newburyport has given some presidents and many professors. Washington, Lafayette, Talleyrand, have all made some spot in the town famous, one living here, one being entertained here, and one performing his great sleeping-act in a bed in the old Prince House. From here Brissot went back to France to die on the scaffold of the Girondists. Here Whitefield died and lies entombed. Here Parson Milton, that son of thunder, used to make his evening family prayer a pattern for preachers: "O Lord! keep us this night from the assassin, the incendiary, and the devil, for Christ's sake, amen." Here the weighty jurist Theophilus Parsons was born and bred; here John Quincy Adams and Rufus King studied law; here Cushing rose, and Garrison, and Gough; here the great giver George Peabody once dwelt and often came; here John Pierrepont wrote his best verses; here the artist Bricher first found inspiration; here Harriet Livermore, that ardent missionary of the East whom "Snowbound" celebrates, was born; here the Lowells sprang; hardly more than a gunshot off, on one side, is the ancestral home of the Longfellows, and, on the other, Whittier lives and sings. Here, also, has been the home of various inventors of renown; the compressibility of water was here discovered; here steel engraving by a simple and beautiful process was invented; here the machine for making nails, which had previously been painfully hammered out one by one; here an instrument for measuring the speed with which a ship goes through the sea, and here a new span for timber bridges, used now on most of our larger rivers, bridging the Merrimack, Kennebec, Connecticut, and Schuylkill; almost every mechanic, indeed, has some fancy on which he spends his leisure, one amusing himself with making the delicate calculations necessary, and then just as delicately burnishing brazen reflectors for telescopes, before his heart was broken by those refractors with which Safford and Tuttle (both connected with the town) have swept the sky; another occupying himself, to the neglect of business, with the model of a machine in which all his soul was rapt, and which, unknown to him, an ancient had invented a couple of thousand years ago, while others are busy with the more useful low-water reporters, and with those improvements in the manufacture of tobacco which have all sprung from a son of the town. It is in mechanics that Newburyport has always excelled; her shipyards once lined all the water-side there, shortly after the Revolution, wishing to export lumber, and having but few ships, she bound the lumber together in firm rafts, with a cavity in the centre for provisions and possible shelter, and furnishing them with secure though rude sailing apparatus, consigned them to the winds and waves, and after voyages of twenty-six days they were registered in their ports on the other side of the Atlantic; but before that experiment her ships were, and they still are, models to the whole world, for here were launched those fleetest clippers that ever cut the wave, the Dreadnaught and the Racer,

They go out, but they never come back; great East Indiamen no longer ride at anchor in her offing as they used to do; the bar of the Merrimack, which once in about a hundred years accumulates into such an insuperable obstacle that the waters find a new channel, is a foe they do not care to face when once piloted safely over its white line; and, though many things have been done with piers, and buoys, and a breakwater built by Government and crushed like a toy by the next storm, it still binds its spell about Newburyport commerce. Possibly if, by any other magic, the town could ever grow sufficiently to require the filling up of the flats, then the stream, inclosed in a narrower and deeper channel, would find sufficient force to drive before it the envious sands which now the Cape Ann currents sweep into its mouth.

Nevertheless, the bar alone is not adequate to account for the financial misfortunes of the town; ships go up to New Orleans over much more dangerous waters; and the Embargo of the early part of the century bears by far the greater responsibility. Then the great hulks rotted at the wharves unused, with tar-barrels, which the angry sailors called Madison's Nightcaps, inverted over the topmasts to save the rigging, while their crews patrolled the streets in riotous and hungry bands, and observed the first anniversary of the Embargo Act with tolling bells, minute-guns, flags at half-mast, and a procession with muffled drums and crapes. Perhaps it was owing to this state of feeling in the town that the old slanders of her showing blue-lights to the befogged enemy arose. Together with the Embargo came the Great Fire; every wooden town has suffered a conflagration, and Newburyport has always been a prey to the incendiary; but her celebrated fire broke out on a spring night some sixty years ago, when nearly every one was wrapped in the first slumber, and spread with the speed of the lightnings over a track of more than sixteen acres, in the most compact and wealthy portion of the town. Such an immense property was destroyed that the whole place was impoverished; many families were totally beggared; people hurried to the scene from a dozen miles away; women passed the buckets in the ranks, and helpless crowds swung to and fro in the thoroughfares. The spectacle is described by an old chronicle as having been terribly sublime; the wind, changing, blew strongly, and drove the flames in fresh directions, where they leaped in awful columns high into the air, and stretched a sheet of fire from street to street; the moon became obscured in the murky atmosphere that hung above the town, but the town itself was lighted as brilliantly as by day, and the heat melted the glass in the windows of houses not destroyed; while the crash of falling walls, the roaring of chimneys like distant thunder, the volumes of flames wallowing upward from the ruins and filling the air with a shower of fire into which the birds fluttered and dropped, the weird reflection in the river, the lowing of the cattle, the cries of distress from the people, made the scene cruelly memorable; and though afterward that portion of the town was rebuilt with brick, Newburyport never recovered from the shock and loss. Some years subsequently a boy of seventeen was convicted of another arson, and in spite of much exertion to the contrary, expiated the penalty of the law. But

a flaming Nemesis fell upon the town, perhaps for having allowed the boy's execution, and ever since that time other incendiaries, emulous of his example, have constantly made it their victim; one, in particular, being so frequent in his attempts, that on a windy or stormy night the blaze was so sure to burst forth that the citizens could not sleep in their beds; he appeared to be the subject of a mania for burning churches, almost all of the sixteen in town having been fired, sometimes two together, and on several occasions successfully; and no dweller in Newburyport will easily forget the night on which the old North Church was burned, when every flake of the wild snow-storm seemed to be a spark of fire, and more than one superstitious wretch, plunging out into the gale, could find no centre to the universal glare, and shuddered with fright in belief that the Day of Judgment had come at last.

But one extraordinary thing or another is always happening in Newburyport; if it is not a fire, it is a gale; and if it is not a gale, it is an earthquake. The situation of the town is very fine. As you approach it by land, bleak fields and lichened boulders warn you of the inhospitable sea-coast; but once past their barrier, and you are in the midst of gardens. The town lies on a gentle hillside, with such slope and gravelly bottom that an hour after the heaviest rains its streets afford good walking. Behind it lies an excellent glacial moraine and a champaign country, shut in by low hills, and once, most probably, the bed of the river. Its adjacent territory is netted in rivers and rivulets; the broad Merrimack, with its weird and strange estuary, imprisoned by Plum Island; the Artichoke, a succession of pools lying in soft, semi-shadows beneath the overhanging growth of beech and oak, and feathery elms lighting the darker masses, each pool enfolded in such wise that one sees no outlet, but slides along with the slow tide, lifts a bough, and slips into the next, where some white-stemmed birch perhaps sends a perpetual rustle through the slumberous air, a wild grape-vine climbs from branch to branch, or an early reddening tupelo shakes its gay mantle in the scattered sun, and with its reflex in the dark transparency, wakens one from half the sleepy spell of the enchantment there; these streams, with the Quascacunquen or Parker, the Little, Powwow, Back, and Rowley rivers, with their slender, but foaming black and white affluents, all make it a place of meadows; and he who desires to see a meadow in perfection, full of emerald and golden tints, and claret shadows, withdrawing into distance till lost in the sparkle of the sea, must seek it here, where Heade found material for his exquisite and dainty marsh and meadow views.

The scenery around the town, it may thus be imagined, is something of unusual beauty; on one side are to be had the deciduous woods of the Stackyard Gate, where the carriage-wheels crackle through winding miles of fragrant brake and fern, and on the other the stately pines and hemlocks of Follymill, the air sweet as an orange-grove with resinous perfume, while the river-road to Haverhill, with West Amesbury swathed in azure mist upon the opposite hill, and sapphire reaches of the stream unfolding one after another, is a series of raptures. The people, well acquainted with the beauty that surrounds them, are very fond of their chief river; it is the scene of frolicking the summer long, and in winter its black and ice-edged tides seem to be the only pulses of the frozen town. To some the life upon this river is only play, to others it is deadly earnest, for a large portion of those who live along the banks on the Water street, the most picturesque of the highways, are fishermen and their households, familiar with all the dangers of the seas—the babies there rocked in a dory, the men, sooner or later, wrecked upon the Georges; meanwhile the men mackerel all summer down in the Bay of Chaleurs, pilot off and on the coast dark nights and dreary days, run the bar and the breakers with a storm following the keel; many of them, as they advance in life, leave their seafaring and settle down at shoe-making, or buy a plot of land and farm it in an untaught way, but just as many find their last home in a grave rolled between two waves.

When a storm comes up, and the fog-banks sweep in from sea, hiding the ray of the twin harbor-lights, and the rote upon the beach-which every night is heard through the quiet streets beating like a heart, swells into a sullen and unbroken roar—when the shipyards are afloat, the water running breast-high across the wharves, the angry tides rising knee-deep in the lower lanes, and the spray tossed over the tops of the houses there whose foundations begin to tremble and whose dwellers fly for safety, then the well-sheltered people up in the remote High street, where nothing is known of the storm but the elms tossing their boughs about, may have sorry fancies of some vessel driving on Plum Island, of parting decks and of unpitied cries in the horror of blackness and breaker—may even hear the minute-guns in pauses of the gale; but the stress of weather falls upon the homes and hearts of these watchers on the Water street, for to them each swell and burst of the blast means danger to their own roof and the life snatched from a husband's or a father's lips. Mrs. E. Vale Smith in her history of Newburyport makes thrilling mention of these storms, with the wrecks of the Primrose, the Pocahontas, the Argus, and others, and every resident of the place has had before his eyes the picture which she draws of "the heavy moaning of the sea—a bark vainly striving to clear the breakers—blinding snow—a slippery deck—stiff and glazed ropes—hoarse commands that the cruel winds seize and carry far away from the ear of the sailor—a crash of tons of falling water beating in the hatches—shrieks which no man heard, and ghastly corpses on the deceitful, shifting sands, and the great ocean-cemetery still holding in awful silence the lost bodies of the dead." Such things, of course, make the place the home of romance, and Mr. George Lunt, a poet of no mean pretensions and a native of the town, has founded his novel of "Eastford" on the incidents its daily life affords.

Newburyport has also known the effects of other convulsions of nature; a hailstorm, with a deposit twelve inches in depth, is still spoken of there, together with snow-storms tunneled from door to door, a northeaster that blew the spray of the sea a dozen miles inland and loaded the orchard boughs with salt crystals, and whirlwinds mighty enough to blow down

one meeting-house and to lift another with all the people in it and set it in a different spot—whirlwinds coming a quarter of a century too soon, as, if they had but moved a meeting-house there at a later day, a parish would not have been so divided on the question of location as straightway to become, one-half of them, Episcopalians for whom Queen Anne endowed a chapel. But worse than whirlwinds, storms, fires, or the devastating yellow-fever that once nearly decimated the place, were the earth-quakes that for more than a hundred years, at one period, held high carnival there, and are still occasionally felt. The first of these oc-curred in 1638, on the noon of a summer day, as the colonists, assembled in town-meeting, were discussing their unfledged affairs. We can well imagine their consternation, just three years established, their houses built, woods felled, fields largely cleared, and the June corn just greenly springing up, to find that their en-campment on this spot, so rich in soil, so con-venient to the sea, so well guarded from the Indian, had left them the prey to an enemy whose terrors were so much worse than all others in the degree in which they partook of the dark, unknown, and infinite. It was not long before another earthquake followed the first. Its trembling and vibration and sudden shocks preceded, as that had been, by a roar like the bursting of great guns, while birds for-sook their nests, dogs howled, and the whole brute creation manifested the extreme of terror; by-and-by there came one that lasted a week, with six or eight shocks a day, then one where the shocks were repeated for half an hour with-out any cessation, and presently others where the ground opened and left fissures a foot in width, where sailors on the coast supposed their vessels to have struck, the sea roared and swelled, flashes of fire ran along the ground, amazing noises were heard like peals and claps of thunder, walls and chimneys fell, cellars opened, floating islands were formed, springs were made dry in one site and burst out in an-other, and tons of fine white sand were thrown up, which, being cast upon the coals, burnt like brimstone. Various causes have been assigned to these earthquakes, not the least absurd of which was the supposition of a cave reaching from the sea to the headwaters of the Merri-mack, filled with gases, into which the high tides rushing made the occurrence of the phenomena; but as they have always appeared in connection with more tremendous disturb-ances in other parts of the world, it is probable that they are but the same pulsations of the old earth's arteries, felt in Vesuvius or Peru with more terrible effect. Although there have been more than two hundred of these convul-sions, nobody was ever seriously injured by their means, and so used to them did the peo-ple become, that finally they are spoken of in their records merely as "the earthquake," as one would speak of any natural event, of the tide or of the moon. For the last century, however, their outbursts have been of very in-frequent occurrence, and have nowise marred the repose of the sweet old place, which now and then awakens to storm or fever sufficient to prevent stagnation, but for the most part slumbers on serenely by its riverside, the ideal of a large and ancient country-town, peaceful enough, and almost beautiful enough, for Par-adise.

DOVER.

A DOZEN miles above Portsmouth lies the old town of Dover, on the route to the White Mountains, which hills, as it has been said, were first explored by a party from the place, and always previously believed (both by the Indians and many of the settlers) to be haunted by powerful and splendid spirits. Dover is the oldest town in the State, and though Portsmouth may have the first church-organ, Dover has the honor of having possessed the first church-edifice, strongly palisaded in the days of primitive worship there. This town is the Cocheco of the early settlers, and is situated upon a stream of that name, a branch of the Piscataqua, which by its cascades—one of more than thirty-two feet—offered good opportunity of mill-sites to the first fellers of the forest, allowing them to clear their ground and manufacture their lumber at once. Of these opportunities later generations have not been slow to take advantage, and the flow of water now turns the ponderous machinery of multitudes of looms, the yards of whose manufacture are numbered only by millions, while an enormous backwater exists in the reserve of the neighboring town of Strafford, sufficient at any time to drown out a drouth.

Of all the manufacturing towns of New England, Dover is one of the most picturesque, and, from some of the loftier points within its limits, meadow, lake, river and phantom mountain-ranges combine to make a varied view of pastoral beauty. But there are other views to the full as interesting for the lover of humanity, when at night all the mill-windows blaze out and are repeated in the river, or when at noon the thousands of operatives pour forth from the factory-gates, and busy Peace seems half disguised. Still it is Peace, and Prosperity beside her; and much it would amaze some ghost of the dead and gone could he, without losing his thin and impalpable essence altogether, obtain a noonday glimpse of the scene of his old troubles. For the place has not been in the past a haunt of Peace—from the time, during the last war with England, when the ships, kept from going to sea by the American powers, were drawn up the river to Dover lest they should be destroyed at the wharves of Portsmouth by the British powers, to the time, a hundred and seventy-five years

before, when the followers of Mrs. Ann Hutchinson, with their Antinomian heresies, stirred up sedition among a people for whose preservation from English tyranny on the one hand, and Indian cruelty on the other, perfect unanimity of heart and mind was necessary—with all the troubles in the meantime occasioned by Mason, who made claim, by royal grant, to the land the settlers had purchased of the Aborigines and all the troubles with the Aborigines themselves.

Dover is more peculiarly the scene of the old Indian outrages than any other New England town can be considered, inasmuch as it was not only there that the famous Waldron Massacre occurred, but the place was also the stage of most of the events that, during a dozen years, led up to that terrific night's work, and that constitute a bit of interesting history never faithfully written out, and which now probably never will be, several of the links being lost, and remaining only to be conjectured from their probabilities.

In 1640 there were four distinct settlements on the Piscataqua and its confluent streams; but each having an individual and voluntary management, and all of them being too much divided in opinion to establish a government of mutual concessions among themselves, and hope of any protection from the King, then in sorry plight himself, being out of the question, the four settlements agreed in one thing, and unanimously requested permission to come under the jurisdiction of the Massachusetts Colony—a request very gladly granted, as, while reserving rights of property to the owners, it afforded that Colony better opportunity to establish the boundaries, three miles north of the Merrimack at any branch thereof, which she had always claimed; and in return for this opportunity she allowed deputies who were not Church-members to sit in the General Court—a privilege she had not given her own people, but which was perhaps necessary where but few, as in New Hampshire, were of the Puritan persuasion. Under this arrangement, Richard Waldron was for more than twenty years a deputy, and several years Speaker of the Assembly; he was also a Justice, and the Sergeant-Major of the Militia in that part of the country; and when the connection with

Massachusetts had been severed, be was, for a time, the Chief Magistrate of the Province. He had married in England; and, being a person of some wealth, on his arrival here he had bought large tracts of land, received large grants for improvement, had built the first saw-mill on the Cocheco, followed it with others, and established a trading-post with the Indians. He was evidently a man of remarkable character, respected by his neighbors for his uprightness, and everywhere for his ability.

Whatever he did was done with a will; as a magistrate he persecuted the Quakers to the extent of the law, though he was known to shed tears when passing sentence of death upon an offender; as a landlord he fought the claims of Mason and his minions persistently, being thrice suspended from the Council, and twice sentenced to fines which he paid only after an arrest of his body; while as a soldier he was no less zealous in behalf of the public interest than in private capacity he had proved himself in behalf of his own. He appears to have exercised a certain fascination on the Indians of the locality, being able for many years to do with them as he would, and Cocheco having long been spared by them when the war-whoop resounded over almost every other settlement in the land—a circumstance aptly illustrating the adage that things are what you make them, since, so long as the Indians were treated like brothers, they fulfilled the law of love, in rude but faithful manner; but once trapped like wild beasts, and wild beasts they became.

These Indians were chiefly the Pennacooks, a tribe belonging to the region of the Merrimack and its tributaries, who traded their pelts at Waldron's post for ammunition, blankets, fineries, and such articles as they were allowed to have, and who on more than one occasion showed their capability for gratitude just as strongly as they subsequently showed it for revenge. They sometimes took advantage of Waldron's absence to procure from his partner the liquor which he would not sell to them; but in the main they seemed to have a wholesome fear of him, not unmixed with affection and trust in his honor. . This tribe had been almost annihilated by the Mohawks, or Men-eaters, of whom they entertained a deadly terror, and by an ensuing pestilence; and being once accused of unfriendly intentions, by messengers sent from the settlements, they did not scruple to disarm suspicion by betraying their own weakness, and averring that they consisted of only twenty-four warriors, with their squaws and pappooses; while their wise old sachem, Passaconaway, whose people believed that he could make water burn, raise a green leaf from the ashes of a dry one, and metamorphose himself into a living flame, had early seen the futility of attempts upon the English, had always advised his subjects to peace, and had imbued his son, Wonnelancet, so strongly with his opinions, that the latter never varied his rule from that which his father's had been. When the war with King Philip of the Wampanoags broke out, a body of soldiery was sent to the Pennacooks to ascertain the part they intended to play; but seeing so large a company approaching, the Indians, who had had no idea of joining the war, concealed themselves; upon which, in

mere wantonness, the soldiery burned their wigwams and provisions. Instead of revenging this injury, they only withdrew further away, to the headwaters of the Connecticut, and passed a quiet winter in their usual pursuits. In the meanwhile, however, the other tribes—Tarratines, Ossipees, and Pequawkets—became restless, and presently commenced hostilities upon the outlying points; and Falmouth, Saco, Scarborough, Wells, Woolwich, Kittery, Durham, Salmon Falls, and other spots, were red with slaughters, and in three months eighty men were killed between the Piscataqua and the Kennebec. With the winter there came a tremendous fall of snow, and that, together with the severity of the season and the famine that distressed them, occasioned these Indians to sue for peace; and, coming to Major Waldron, they expressed sorrow for their conduct, and made repeated promises of better behavior for the future. But, this being done, the survivors among King Philip's men, who, at his death, leaving total extirpation, had fled from their own forests and disseminated themselves among the northern tribes, inflamed them anew with memory of wrong and outrage, endured doubtless, as well as committed, and the hostilities began again by a demonstration at Falmouth, and were continued, the savages burning the homesteads as the dwellers abandoned them, till between Casco Bay and the Penobscot not a single English settlement was left. At this time, the Pennacooks, who had not been concerned in the butcheries at all, seem to have been used by Major Waldron to secure a peace which he almost despaired of obtaining in any other way; and it was through their agency, it may be supposed, that some four hundred of the Eastern Indians, of all tribes, with their women and children, assembled in Cocheco, on the 6th of September, 1676, to sign a full treaty of peace with Major Waldron, whom, the historian Belknap says, they looked upon as a friend and father.

At this instant a body of soldiery, that had been dispatched to the northward, with orders to report to Major Waldron, the various settlements on their way being directed to reinforce them as they might be able, arrived at Cocheco; and, obediently to the instructions which they brought, Major Waldron had no choice but to surround and seize the whole four hundred of the confiding Indians.

To Major Waldron this must have been an exceedingly trying moment: his plighted word, his honor, his friendship for this poor people whom he knew so well, all his sentiments as a man and a Christian, must have drawn him one way, while his duty as a soldier compelled him the other. To resign his command in the face of the enemy and under such instructions would doubtless have involved him in most serious difficulties; to disobey these instructions imposed upon him a too fearful responsibility in case of future depredations by those whom he should have spared against his orders; he was a soldier, and his first duty was obedience; and, for the rest, the young captains of the force sent by the Governor were on fire with eagerness, and it was with difficulty he could restrain their martial spirit while he took counsel with himself. In this strait the Major unfortunately thought of a stratagem that might be used, and having, it is said, assured the Indians, who had been a little alarmed by the arrival of the soldiery, that they had nothing to apprehend, he proposed to them a sham fight with powder, but without balls, and on the signal of the discharge of their guns —making that a pretext for considering that the Indians had violated the understanding—the soldiery surrounded them, by an actual military movement, and with one or two exceptions made prisoners of the whole body. One of these exceptions was a young Indian who, escaping, sought and found refuge with Mrs. Elizabeth Heard, and in his thankfulness promised her a recompense of future safety, and one day redeemed the pledge.

Although the Pennacooks were immediately separated from the other prisoners and discharged, upon which Major Waldron had perhaps relied for his own exculpation with them, and only half of the whole number were sent to Boston, where some six or eight, being convicted of old murders, were hanged, and the rest sold into foreign slavery, yet they, together with all other Indians both far and near, regarded it as a treachery upon Major Waldron's part that absolved them from all ties and demanded a bitter reparation. It is said that there is no sufficient evidence of their having been invited to treat for more definite peace, and that they had no guarantee of protection in their assemblage at Cocheco ; but the mere tact of their quiet presence in that number, an unusual if not unprecedented thing with them, implies that the occasion was a special one, and that they must have had Major Waldron's verbal promise of safety at least, while, if it had been otherwise, it would have been absurd and impossible for them to regard the affair as so signal and abominable a treachery of his, worthy to be remembered with such undying hatred and expiated in his own person with such torture. This view of the facts is fortified, moreover, by the subsequent action of the Pennacooks. That they should have fancied themselves so peculiarly aggrieved as they did, should so long in all their wanderings have cherished their rancor, and should at last have executed vengeance through their own tribe, in itself testifies sufficiently that they had been used by Major Waldron to allure the other Indians into the treaty under promises of protection, and felt the course which they pursued to be a necessary vindication of their honor as well as a gratification of their passions.

They were not, however, in any situation to pay their debt at once, and on being set at liberty they withdrew to their hunting-grounds, and as season after season rolled away had apparently forgotten all about it. A grandson of old Passaconaway at last ruled them—Kancamagus, sometimes called John Hagkins. He was a chief of different spirit from the previous sachems, and the injuries his people had received from the English rankled in his remembrance ; his thinned and suffering tribe, his stolen lands, his old wrongs, were perpetual stings ; and when finally the English, dispatching emissaries to the Mohawks, engaged their co-operation against the Eastern Indians, nothing but impotence restrained his wrath. It is possible that even then, by reason of his distresses, he might have been appeased, if the English could ever have been brought to consider that the Indian's nature was human nature, and to treat him with anything but violence when he was strong and contempt when he was weak. Several letters which Kancamagus sent to the Governor of New Hampshire, and which are curiosities, are adduced to prove his amenable disposition at this time :

"MAY 15th, 1685.

"Honor Governor my friend You my friend. I desire your worship and your power, because I hope you can do some great matters—this one. I am poor and naked and I have no men at my place because I afraid allways Mohogs he will kill me every day and night. If your worship when please pray help me you no let Mohogs kill me at my place at Malamake Rever called Panakkog and Natukkog, I will submit your worship and your power.—And now I want pouder and such alminishun, shatt and guns, because I have forth at my home and I plant theare.

"This all Indian hand, but pray you do consider your humble servant, JOHN HAGKINS."

This letter was written for Kancamagus by an Indian teacher, who signed it, together with King Hary, Old Robin, Mr. Jorge Rodannonukgus, and some dozen others, by making their respective marks. The next letter is a much more complicated affair in style ; it is dated on the same day.

"Honor Mr. Governor:

"Now this day I com your house, I want se you, and I bring my hand at before you I want shake hand to you if your worship when please then you receive my hand then shake your hand and my hand. You my friend because I remember at old time when live my grant father and grant mother then Englishmen com this country, then my grant father and English-men they make a good govenant, they friend allwayes, my grant father leving at place called Malamake Rever. other name chef Natukkog and Panukkog, that one rever great many names, and I bring you this few skins at this first time I will give you my friend. This all Indian hand. JOHN HAWKINS, Sagamore."

These letters winning no notice from the contemptuous official, on the same day were followed by another :

"Please your Worship—I will intreat you matther, you my friend now ; this, if my Indian he do you long, pray you no put your law, because som my Indians fooll, some men much love drunk then he no know what he do, maybe he do mischif when he drunk, if so pray you must let me know what he done because I will ponis him what have done, you, you my friend, if you desire my business then sent me I will help you if I can. Mr. JOHN HOGKINS."

None of these letters having produced any effect, the sachem abandoned the one-sided correspondence, and on the next morning indited another epistle to Mr. Mason, the claimant of the Province.

"Mr. Mason - Pray I want speake you a few words if your worship when please, because I com parfas. I will speake this governor but he go away so he say at last night, and so far I understand this governor his power that your power now, so he speak his own mouth. Pray if you take what I want pray come to me because I want go hom at this day.

"Your humble servant,

JOHN HAGKINS, Indian Sogmon."

There was something touching in these letters, to any but an early settler; but apparently they were quite disregarded, and Kancamagus had every right to feel ill-used by the neglect which his petition for protection from the Mohawks met, and it is probable that this waiting at rich men's gates only deepened the old grudge. At the close of the summer various affronts were put upon the settlers at Saco, and their dogs were killed; after which the Indians gathered their own corn and removed their families to some unknown place. This resembling a warlike menace, messengers were sent, to discover its meaning, who were informed that the Pennacooks had received threats from the Mohawks, and had withdrawn from the settlements that the English might not suffer on their account—far too plausible a reply and too magnanimous action for the truth. But an agreement of friendship was then made, and was signed, among the rest, by Kancamagus and another chief named Mesandouit.

Kancamagus had no intention of making this anything but a brief truce, and he improved the time to gather around himself the little band of the sullen Pennacooks, and to strike hands with the Pequawkets, and the remnant of the more northerly tribes, while several of the Strange Indians, who were among the four hundred prisoners of that 6th of September, escaped from their slavery, returned to New England, found their way to the haunts of the Pennacooks and Ossipees, and with the recital of their sufferings assisted him in fanning the steadily smoldering fires of hate to a fury against their betrayer on that unforgotten day.

Nor had Major Waldron endeavored at all to pacify the Indians, in the meantime. His prominent position alone would have kept his great misdeed fresh in their remembrance, even without his accustomed hot-headed energy of action. No little act of his that could embitter one savage remained untold by another; they fancied deceit in all his dealings now, and used to tell that in buying their peltry he would say his own hand weighed a pound, and would lay it on the other scale. He had been in command, too, on a frontier expedition, where, a conference being held with arms laid aside, Waldron, suspecting foul play, seized the point of a lance which he espied hid beneath a board, and, drawing it forth, advanced brandishing it toward the other party, who had probably concealed it there to be used only in case of a second act of treachery on his own part, and the conference broke up in a skirmish, in which several of the Indians, including a powerful chieftain, were killed, a canoe-full drowned, and five were captured, together with a thousand pounds of dried beef —and another mark was made on the great score which at some time the Indians meant to cross out.

Sir Edmund Andros was the Governor of New England now, and in the spring of 1688, fired with ambitious projects or with cupidity, he sailed down the coast in a man-o'-war, and failing to achieve any other doughty action, plundered, in the absence of its master, the house of the Baron de St. Castine, a French officer, who had married the daughter of the great Tarratine chief, Modokawando. Castine, burning with indignation, immediately used all his influence, and it was great, to excite the Indians to avenge the injury and insult; and from unheeded complaints that their fisheries were obstructed, their corn devoured by cattle, their lands patented without consent, and their trading accounts tampered with, they proceeded to reprisal, and the old difficulties broke out afresh. They were all at an end, however, before the next summer. The crops were in the Indians went peaceably to and fro through the settlements, their wrongs seemed to be righted, their wounds to be healed; thirteen years had elapsed since the capture of the four hundred, the settlers no longer remembered it, the Indians themselves never made allusion to it; Waldron, now nearly eighty years old, but full of vigor, relied securely on his power over the savages, his acquaintance with their character, and his long-acknowledged superiority; the village, with its five garrison-houses, into which the neighboring families withdrew at night, but kept no watch, feeling safe behind the bolted gates of the great timber walls, reposed in an atmosphere of tranquillity and contentment, and no one suspected any guile.

It was while affairs were in this comfortable condition that, on the 27th of June, 1689, the Indians were observed rambling through the town, on one errand and another, in far more frequent numbers than usual or than seemed necessary for trade. Many strange faces were among them; and it was noticed that their sidelong glances scrutinized the defenses very closely. To more than one housewife a kindly squaw muttered hints of mischief, but so darkly as to give only a vague sense of danger. As night drew near, one or two of the people, a little alarmed, whispered to Major Waldron a fear that evil was in the air. Waldron laughed at them, told them to go and plant their pumpkins, and he would let them know when the Indians were going to break out; and being warned again at a later hour by a young man, who assured him there was great uneasiness in the settlement, he said he knew the Indians perfectly, and there was not the least occasion for concern. That night the sachem, Mesandouit, was hospitably entertained at Waldron's table. "Brother Waldron," said he, "what would you do if the Strange Indians were to come now?" and Waldron carelessly answered that he could assemble a hundred men by the lifting of his finger. It is not said whether Mesandouit remained in the garrison-house or not; but on the same evening a couple of squaws requested a night's lodging on the hearth, telling the Major that a company of Indians were encamped a few miles off, who were coming to trade their beaver on the next day. Several of the household objected to the society of the squaws that night, but it being dull weather, Waldron compassionately said, "Let the poor creatures lodge by the fire;" and by-and-by, in total unsuspicion, setting no watch, and thinking no harm, the family retired to bed, while at three of the remaining garrison-houses other squaws had obtained entrance and shelter on a similar pretense.

Five days before, Major Hinchman, of Chelmsford, having heard from two friendly Indians a strange story of hostile intentions against Cocheco, had dispatched an urgent letter to the Governor acquainting him with the rumor.

At the same time, he wrote to Mr. Danforth of the Council, and Mr. Danforth instantly forwarded the letter, and begged the Governor to lose no time, but to send to Cocheco "on purpose rather than not at all;" yet for some unexplained reason—whether the Governor regarded the rumor as idle, or could do nothing till his Council could be gathered—although Major Hinchman's letter was dated on the 22d of June—it was not till the 27th that any attempt was made to apprise Waldron of his danger.

"BOSTON, 27th June, 1689.

"HONORABLE SIR—The Governor and Council having this day received a letter from Major Hinchman, of Chelmsford, that some Indians are come into them, who report that there is a gathering of Indians in or about Pennacook, with design of mischief to the English. Among the said Indians one Hawkins is said to be a principal designer, and that they have a particular design against yourself and Mr. Peter Coffin, which the Council thought it necessary presently to dispatch advice thereof, to give you notice, that you take care of your own safeguard, they intending to endeavor to betray you on a pretension of trade.

"Please forthwith to signify the import hereof to Mr. Coffin and others, as you shall think necessary, and advise of what information you may at any time receive of the Indians' motions.

"By order in Council,

"ISA ADDINGTON, Sec'y.

"To Major Richard Waldron and Mr. Peter Coffin, or either of them, at Cocheco; these with all possible speed."

"THE INDIANS STOLE OFF IN THE MORNING AND LEFT THE LITTLE GRANDDAUGHTER OF MAJOR WALDRON COVERED BY THE SNOW, ALONE IN THE WOODS WITH THE WILD BEASTS AND HUNGER."

The speed, however, came too late. When Mr. Weare, the bearer of this agitated and ill-written letter, on the night of its date reached Newbury, a freshet had swollen the stream so that it was impassable; and while he was riding up and down the bank the squaws had been admitted into the garrison-houses and had stretched themselves before the fires. These squaws had asked in an incidental way to be told how to go out if they should wish to leave the place after the others were asleep, and had willingly been shown the way; and accordingly in the dead of the night, noiselessly as the coming of darkness itself, the bolts were withdrawn by them, and a low whistle crept out into the thickets and the ambush of the river-banks, and sounding their dreadful war-whoop in reply, the Indians leaped within the gates. The squaws, who had faithfully informed themselves, hurriedly signified the number of people in each apartment, and the invaders divided in every direction, and missed none of those they sought. Waldron himself lodged in an inner room, and, wakened by the noise, he leaped out of bed crying, "What now! what now!" and, seizing only his sword, met the Indians, and, old as he was, with his white wrath blazing loftily over the fierce devils, he drove them before him from door to door till he had passed the third. As he sprung back then for other weapons, the Indians rushed up behind him and stunned him with their hatchets, felled him, and dragged him to the hall, where they seated him in an armchair placed on the top of a table, and, tauntingly asking him, "Who shall judge Indians now?" left him to recover his senses while they compelled such of the family as they had spared to prepare them some food. Their hunger being appeased, they returned to Major Waldron, had his books, in which their trade had been registered, brought forth, and as each Indian's turn came, he stepped up, crying, "I cross out my account!" and with his knife drew a deep gash across the breast of the old hero. Tradition adds that, cutting off the hand whose weight they had so often felt, they tossed it into the scales to discover for themselves if indeed it weighed a pound, and were struck with consternation on finding that it did. It is not recorded that Waldron uttered a cry of pain or an entreaty for their mercy. "Oh, Lord!" he said, "oh, Lord!" and, spent with anguish and loss of blood from the shocking mutilation to which he was further subjected, he fell forward on his sword, which one of the tormentors held ready to receive him, and the vengeance that had brooded and waited thirteen years was satisfied.

That night Mrs. Elizabeth Heard, coming up the river with her sons, from Strawberry Bank, was alarmed by the turmoil and the light, and sought protection at Waldron's garrison; but, discovering the terrible state of things there, Mrs. Heard was so prostrated that she had no power to fly, and her children were obliged to leave her—though it would seem as if the three sons might, at least, have dragged her into the shelter of the bushes, where afterward she contrived to crawl. With the daylight an Indian got a glimpse of her, and hastened to part the bushes, pistol in hand, but, looking at her an instant, turned about and left her; he had taken only a stride away when, as if a doubt crossed his mind, he came back, gave her another glance, and with a yell departed. It was

probably the Indian whom she had protected on the day of which this day was the result. Mrs. Heard's own garrison had been saved by the barking of a dog, which wakening William Wentworth—the ancestor of all the Wentworths in this country—he pushed the door to, and, throwing himself on his back, held it with his feet till assistance came, various bullets piercing the oak meanwhile, but missing its valiant and determined old defender. But in two other garrisons the Indians had worked their bloody will; and, having been refused entrance into that of Mr. Coffin's son, they brought out the father, captured at an earlier hour, and threatened the old man's murder before the son's eyes, upon which he also surrendered; but while the house was being plundered, all the Coffins escaped together. After this, setting fire to the mills and houses, the Indians, having killed twenty-two persons and made prisoners of twenty-nine, retreated by the light of the blaze, so rapidly as to be beyond danger before any of the other settlers were aroused to a sense of what had been done.

But in their flight the Indians inaugurated a system that for years continued to plague the settlers—alleviate, though it did, the previous horrors of Indian warfare—and, sparing the lives of their prisoners, they sold them to the French. Among the captives of that night was a little granddaughter of Major Waldron's, who, having been sent by the Indians, while at their dark work in the garrison-house, to bid forth those hiding in another room, had crept into a bed and drawn the clothes about her; she had been found again, though, and had been forced to undertake the march with them, half-clad and on her little bare feet. She was only seven years old, and her trials were bitter.

At one time her master made her stand against a tree while he charged his gun and took aim at her; again, an Indian girl pushed her off a precipice into the river, and, having clambered out, she dared not tell, when questioned, the reason of her being so wet; once the Indians stole off in the morning and left her, covered by the snow, alone in the woods with the wild beasts and hunger, and, tracing them by their foot-prints, the poor little thing went crying after them through the wilderness; and at another time, building a great fire, they told her she was to be ro sted, whereupon bursting into tears she ran and threw her arms round her master's neck, begging him to save her, which, on the condition that she would behave well, he promised her to do. Another capture of more subsequent importance was the wife of Richard Otis, the ancestress of Hon. John Wentworth, of Illinois, and of Mr. Charles Tuttle, late of the Cambridge Observatory. The unhappy Mrs. Otis had seen her husband killed as he rose in bed, a son share his father's fate, a daughter's brains beaten out against the stairs, and with her little daughter Judith, who was subsequently rescued, and her baby of three months old, she was led up through the White Mountain Notch to Canada. This infant of three months became a personage of great interest in her day. Baptized by the French priests and given the name of Christine, and intended by them for conventual life, on reaching maturity she declined taking the vail, and was married to a Frenchman by the name of Le Beau. Upon her husband's death an inextinguishable desire to see her native land took control of her, and not being permitted to carry her children with her, she left them in the hands of friends, upon the liberation of prisoners, and at the loss of all her estate, which was not inconsiderable, as she herself says, journeyed back to Dover. A few years afterward she returned to Canada, where she appears to have been greatly valued, made an unsuccessful effort to recover her children, and again underwent the hardships of the perilous pilgrimage home. She must have been a woman of rather remarkable nature to prefer the New England wilds with their discomforts to the comparatively sumptuous life of the French in Canada ; but she was still young, and whether from pure preference, or because she formed another attachment there at an early date, she remained in New England and married the adventurous Captain Thomas Baker, **who** had himself been a captive of the Indians some years previously, and who had accompanied her on the voyage home ; and, abjuring the religion of her baptism, she embraced the Protestant faith. Her apostasy appeared greatly to distress the priest whose especial charge she had been, and more than a dozen years after her return led to quite a controversial tilt between representatives of the two forms of belief—Father Seguenot addressing her a long and affectionate letter, in which he made her and her husband handsome promises if they would go to Montreal, wrought upon her feelings in describing the death of her **daughter**, set forth quite ably the distinctive **doctrines** of his Church and besought her **to return** to it :

"Let us add, dear Christiné," said he, "that the strange land in which you are **does not** afford you the Paschal Lamb, the true and heavenly manna, the bread of angels ; I mean Jesus Christ contained really within the holy Eucharist, which is only to be found in the Catholic Church ; so that you are in that place, like the prodigal son, reduced to feed on improper and insipid food, which cannot give you life, after having fed here on the most exquisite, most savory, and most delicious food of Heaven—I mean the adorable body and precious b'ood of Jesus Christ at the holy sacrament of the altar." By this letter, written in a crabbed and almost illegible hand, but in the language of her childhood and of countless dear associations, Christiné seems to have been unshaken, and Governor Burnett made a learned and masterly reply to it, among other things declaring, in reference to the passage quoted, that the upholders of this interpretation of the Eucharist did, in St. Paul's words, "crucify to themselves the Son of God afresh and put him to an open shame." These letters attracted much attention throughout the Colonies, and rendered Christiné a person of importance during all her life of nearly ninety years, and **she** received many favors and several grants of land, one of five hundred acres under the guardianship of Colonel William Pepperrell.

But though the greater part of that long term of life was passed in Dover, it was untroubled by any foray of the Indians who once had desolated her friends' and father's dwellings. For, having glutted their vengeance, the Pennacooks were content to pay the penalty, to fly from t eir old hunting-grounds, to abandon their territory and their name, to find refuge in Canada and lose themselves among the Indians of the St. Francis, and, except when some solitary wanderer roamed alone by the graves of his fathers, the Pennacooks never again were seen on the pleasant bank of the "winding water" And no one who surveys the busy, bustling town of Dover to-day, would think that less than two hundred years ago it was the scene of such a tragedy as Waldron's Massacre.

PORTSMOUTH.

An hour after leaving Newburyport, having crossed the Merrimack, no longer on the bridge that Blondin refused to walk, the traveler is in Portsmouth, a town which, without possessing the vitality of Newburyport or the world-known traditions of Salem, is in some regards as interesting as either. Few spots in the whole country can boast the primeval grandeur of which it was the possessor, and traces of which are still to be found both in place and people. Being the only seaport of an independent State—for, before our present confederation, New Hampshire was a little Republic, governed by a President and two Houses of Congress—much home wealth naturally centred there, much foreign wealth and many dignitaries were drawn there; and being a provincial capital, for so long a time the home of Presidents and Governors, and afterward a garrisoned and naval place of the United States, its society has always been of the choicest description, and its homes and habits sumptuous. The greater part of the old families have died out or have left the place, but many of their dwellings remain to tell of the degree of splendor which characterized not only their hospitality, but their common life.

The town lies very prettily upon land between several creeks, just where the Piscataqua widens—to meet the sea three miles below—into a harbor of extraordinary but placid picturesqueness. Martin Pring was its first visitor, and after him John Smith, and it was originally part of the Mason and Gorges grant, although Mason bought out Sir Fernando's interest, built a great house, and established the settlement here himself, sending from Dover an explor ng party to the White Mountains, or Crystal Hills, as they were then called, in the hope of adding diamond mines to his possessions. In the first days the central part of the town was known as Strawberry Bank, and so many an aged resident still speaks of it; and by a singular circumstance it happens that nearly all this portion of Portsmouth, containing public buildings, banks, offices, stores and dwellings, is owned in fee by the old North Church, being some twelve acres in the centre of the city, together with thirty-eight acres through which runs the Islington Road, all of it constituting glebe land leased to the present holders for nine hundred and ninety-nine years, and at the expiration of that little term to fall back wi h all its improvements into the hands of the Church, if the Church be still in existence—a prospective wealth bearing favorable comparison with the present wealth of Trinity Church in New York.

The place still does a very fair business for one of its size, Portsmouth lawns and hosiery being known the country over, and its principal rope-walk furnishing nearly all the rigging of the Maine and Massachusetts marine. Many of the well-shaded streets are paved, and there are library and athenæum, fine schools and churches; among the latter, St. John's, succeeding that to which Caroline, the Queen of George the Second, gave altar and pulpit books, communion service, chancel furniture and a silver christening-basin—a stately and interesting edifice, with its mural tablets and the porphyry font taken at the capture of an African city.

Although Portsmouth probably shared the prevailing sentiment of New England to some extent, she was never thoroughly Puritan, having been planted more for mercantile than religious ends, and she is still a young settlement when we read of the profane game of shovel-board being openly played there, and the character of its banqueting and merrymaking has at all times more of the Cavalier than the Roundhead. In 1711 she built an almshouse at an expense of nearly four thousand pounds, a thing contrary to the genius of all Puritanism; and to the honor of Portsmouth be it known that this was not only the first almshouse in this country, but in the whole civilized world. It was in Portsmouth, too, that there was made perhaps the earliest attack on African slavery, by a decision of the local court that it was a thing not to be tolerated, although, having eased their consciences by the declaration and the law—a famous habit not confined to Portsmouth—the good people went on keeping such property in slaves as they chose.

The rank of the early population there was of a much higher social type than could be found in other settlements. There were the Parkers, the gravestone of whose ancestress was recently uncovered, Lady Zerviah Stanley, who made a love-match and escaped to this country from the wrath of h.r father, the Earl of Derby. There are the Chaunceys, immigrants here through the persecutions of Archbishop Laud, sprung of Chauncey de Chauncey, from Chauncey near Amiens in France, who entered England with the Conqueror; their head in this country could trace his noble descent back to Charlemagne, and back to Egbert in the year 800, lineage not exceeded by Queen Victoria's own. There were the families of Pepperrell and Went-

worth, baroneted for illustrious deeds; and there are to be found the first mention of the old names of Langdon, Frost, Newmarch, Cushing, Sheafe, Penhallow, names which revive the traditions of a magnificent hospitality. Here was born Tobias Lear, the friend and secretary of Washington, and his house remains to-day full of mementoes of his chief; there lived John Langdon, first President of the United States Senate; the handsome face of

"SHE HUNG OUT MANY A SIGNAL FROM HER WINDOW FOR THE GOVERNOR TO READ ACROSS THE OPEN SPACE BETWEEN THEIR DWELLINGS."

Madame Scott, the widow of John Hancock, has many a time looked out of that window; there stands the house in which successively lived Jeremiah Mason and Daniel Webster; there the handsome dwelling of Levi Woodbury, and there were born the Blunts, whose charts to-day define the courses of all modern commerce.

Many other mansions of note are still standing. Here on the corner of Daniel and Chapel streets, with its gambrel-roof and lanthern-lights, is the old Warner House, the first brick house of the place, and whose material was brought from Holland; there are still preserved in it the gigantic pair of elk-horns presented to the head of the house by the Indians with whom he traded, and who, out of their skillfully-painted portraits, still look down at the guest who mounts the staircase; there are paintings by Copley hanging in another place within, and on repapering its hall, a few years since, four coatings of paper being removed, a full-length likeness of Governor Phipps on his charger was discovered, together with other life-sized frescoes, of more or less value, of whose existence people of eighty years had never heard; this house ought to be as secure from the fires of Heaven as a person vaccinated by Jenner ought to be from disease, for it has a lightning-rod put up under Dr. Franklin's personal inspection, and the first one used in the State. Fire has destroyed the spacious house where, a hundred years ago, in the midst of guests assembled with all the illumination and cheer of the times, the beautiful Miss Sheafe sat in her bridal-dress waiting for the bridegroom who never came, but who left his great wealth, his love, and his good name, left his bride to her destiny of alternating doubt and terror, and disappeared out of the world for ever. This same fire, or another, has left no mark of the house to which High Sheriff Parker once hurried so hungrily with Ruth Blay's blood upon his hands—a young girl condemned for murdering her child, though afterward found to be innocent; and her reprieve sent forward to arrive only two minutes too late, for she had been driven to the scaffold, clothed in silk and filling the air with her cries, and hurried out of life before the appointed hour because the sheriff feared lest his dinner should cool by waiting. But there still stands the old "Earl of Halifax" inn, shabby enough now, but once a place of Tory revelry and Rebel riot; a house that has had famous guests in its day, for, not to mention the platitude of Washington's and Lafayette's entertainment, here John Hancock had his headquarters, with Elbridge Gerry, Rutledge, and General Knox; here General Sullivan, President of New Hampshire, convened his council; and here, something later, Louis Philippe and his two brothers of Orleans were cared for. On an island in the harbor, whence is seen the wide view of fort and field and lighthouse, and the sea stretching away till the Isles of Shoals and Agamenticus lie in the horizon like clouds, stands the old Prescott mansion, where the Legislature was wont to be entertained, but whose wide-doored hospitality has given place to that of the State, since it is now another almshouse. In Kittery, a sort of suburb of Portsmouth, the garrison-house, two hundred years old, is still shown, and Sir William Pepperrell's residence by the water, with its once deer-stocked park and avenues of

mighty elms; and, on the other side of the river, in Little Harbor, two miles from the business centre, the old house erected by Governor Benning Wentworth, but now passed out of the hands of his family, remains to delight the antiquary. This house, built around three sides of a square, though only two stories in height, contains fifty-two rooms, and looks like an agglomeration of buildings of various dates and styles: in its cellars a troop of horse could be accommodated in time of danger, and here are still kept in order the council-chamber and the billiard-room, with the spinet and buffet and gun-rack of their time, and the halls, finished in oak and exquisitely carved with the year's work of a chisel, are lined with ancient portraits. Here lived and kept a famous table the old Governor Benning Wentworth, as headstrong and self-willed and passionate as any Wentworth of them all. It is told of him that, when long past his sixtieth year, he lost what was left of his heart to pretty Patty Hilton, his maid-servant; and, assembling a great dinner-party round his board, with the Rev. Arthur Brown, when the walnuts and the wine were on, he rang for Patty, who came and stood blushingly beside him, and then, as Governor of New Hampshire, he commanded the clergyman, who had hesitated at his request as a private gentleman, to marry him; and Patty straightway became Lady Wentworth, in the parlance of the day, and carried things with a high hand ever afterward, until, the old Governor dying, she married Colonel Michael Wentworth, who ran through the property and then killed himself, leaving the legacy of his last words: "I have had my cake, and ate it."

These Wentworths were a powerful and hot-blooded race—nothing but the rigor of the law ever stood between them and a purpose; their talent made New Hampshire a power, and for sixty years they furnished her with Governors. On Pleasant street, at the head of Washington, is still to be found the house of Governor John Wentworth, a successor of Benning; old as it is, the plush upon its walls is as fresh as newly-pressed velvet, and valuable portraits of the Governors and their kin a few years since still hung upon them. Into this house, with its pleasant garden running down to the river, once came a bride under circumstances that the customs of to-day would cause us to consider peculiar. It was Frances Deering, the pet and darling of old Sam Wentworth of Boston, and for whom the pretty villages of Francestown and Deering were named. When very young, she was in love with her cousin John, who, on leaving Harvard, went to England, no positive pledge of marriage passing between them; as he delayed there some years, before his return she had married another cousin, Theodore Atkinson by name. Some years subsequently to their marriage, and after a lingering illness, Theodore died. But John had, in the meantime, returned, clothed with honor and with the regalia of Governor, and, finding his cousin a woman of far lovelier appearance than even her lovely youth had promised, had not hesitated to pay her his devoirs, which, the gossips said, she had not hesitated to accept, hanging out many a signal from her window for the Governor to read across the open space between their dwellings. On one day Theodore breathed his last. His burial took place on the following Wednesday; by the Governor's order all the bells in town were tolled, flags were hung at half-mast, and minute-guns were fired from the fort and from the ships-of-war in the harbor. On Sunday the weeping widow, clad in crapes, listened in church to the funeral eulogies; on Monday her affliction was mitigated; on Tuesday all the fingers of all the seamstresses of the country roundabout were flying; and on the next Sunday, in the white satins and jewels and far-dingales of a bride, she walked up the aisle the wife of Governor Wentworth. When the Revolution came, the Governor, a Tory, had to fly; but his wife's beauty won favor at the Court, she was appointed a lady-in-waiting there, and her husband was rewarded for his loyalty to the Crown by the governorship of Nova Scotia, where he held his state till death humbled it.

Portsmouth, it may be seen, abounds in such traditions as these of the Wentworths. Of another sort is the story of Captain Samuel Cutts. He had sent out his vessel to the Spanish coasts, and his clerk, young William Bennett, who had been reared in his counting-room, and who, after the old-fashioned way, made his master's interests his own, went supercargo; the vessel fell among thieves, but thieves who consented to restore their booty upon receipt of several thousand dollars, a sum of much less value than the vessel and cargo. Captain Leigh, of course, had not the money with him, nor did it seem practicable to keep the vessel on full expense while a messenger was sent home for it; but upon condition of leaving hostages he was suffered to sail away, young Bennett and a friend remaining. The terms were carefully impressed on Captain Leigh's memory: so many days and it would be time for the money—till then the hostages were to be well treated; the money not forthcoming, the hostages were to be imprisoned on bread and water; so many days more, and they were to be left unfed till they starved to death. Captain Leigh, to whom Bennett was dear as a son, crowded on all sail for home, arrived, told his story, and, on sacred promise that the money should instantly be paid, delivered the ship that still belonged to her captors into the hands of Captain Samuel Cutts, and waited breathlessly for the promise to be kept. Meanwhile the friend of Bennett had escaped, Bennett himself trusting so in his master's faith that he refused to go. Captain Leigh waited silently a while, but, seeing no prospect of the ransom's being paid, he began to urge the matter—precious time was passing; then Bennett's parents urged, and were assured that the money had been sent. But when, if the money had been sent, it was time for Bennett's return and yet he did not come, anxiety mounted again to fever-heat; there were agonized prayers offered in church by the parents, and Captain Leigh heard them ringing in his ears; he could think of nothing else; he knew the gradations of the cruel days apportioned to Bennett: on such a day he went into solitary confinement; on such a day he was deprived of food; on such a day he must have ceased to live. When that day came, Bennett had truly undergone all his sentence and was dead, and Captain Leigh was mad.

But all the traditions of splendor are not confined to the gentility of Portsmouth. A colored man, steward of a ship sailing from the Piscataqua, went into loftier society than many

of his betters ever saw. He was in a Russian port, during a review held by the Emperor in person, and went on shore, only to attract as much attention as the Emperor himself, for a black skin was rarer than black diamonds there. The next day officials came on board the ship, to learn if the black man's services could be had for the imperial family, and the fortunate fellow left his smoky caboose, hard fare and half-contemptuous companions, to become an object of admiration behind an Emperor's chair; and, being allowed to return to Portsmouth for his wife and children, had the satisfaction of parading his gold-laced grandeur before the humbler citizens to his heart's content.

It is not only in legends of the elegancies of colonial life, however, that Portsmouth is rich. She had her valiant part in all the old French and Indian wars, and the only ship-of-the-line owned by the Continental Government was here constructed, on Badger's Island, where a hundred ships had been built before. Congress having in 1776 ordered her agents to procure, among others, three seventy-four-gun ships, the America was begun, being the heaviest ship that had ever been laid down on the continent. Little was done about her, though, till nearly three years afterward, when John Paul Jones was ordered to command her. Jones came to Portsmouth, found the ship only a skeleton, and, without material or money and in the face of countless obstacles, pushed forward her construction, though declaring it the most tedious and distasteful service he was ever charged with. As soon as the British heard of the progress the ship was making, they devised a thousand plans to destroy her, intelligence of which was constantly furnished to Jones, in cipher; and at last, on an alarm sent by General Washington himself, failing to obtain a guard from New Hampshire, he prevailed upon the carpenters to keep watch by night, and paid them from his own purse; and they were otherwise rewarded by the sight of large whaleboats stealing into the river on muffled oars, and creeping, with their armed companies, up and down by the America, without daring to board her. At the birth of the French Dauphin, Jones mounted artillery in the ship, decorated her with the flags of all nations, fired salutes, gave a great entertainment on board, and after dark illuminated her from truck to keelson, kept up a feu de joie till midnight, and on the anniversary of Independence re-ected his rejoicings. The America was superbly built—both stern and bows made so strong that the men might always be under cover. Her sculpture, also, is said to have been of a noble order: America, at the head, crowned with laurels, one arm raised to heaven, and the other supporting a buckler with thirteen silver stars on a blue ground, while the rest of the person was enveloped in the smoke of war. Other large figures in relief were at the stern and elsewhere, representing Tyranny and Oppression, Neptune, and Mars, and Wisdom surrounded by the lightnings. Jones, however, was destined never to command this ship on which he had lavished so much. The Magnifique, a seventy-four-gun ship of the French, having just been wrecked in Boston Harbor, Congress magnanimously presented to France the only ship-of-the-line in the American possession, and for the tenth time Jones was deprived of a command. Nevertheless, he completed the ship, and at last launched her; the launching being no easy task in that little bay, with the bluff of the opposite shore but a hundred fathoms distant, and ledges of rock and conflicting currents everywhere between. But, letting her slide precisely at high water, dropping the bow anchors and slipping the cable fastened to the ground on the island, at a signal she was off and afloat in safe water, and given over to the late commander of the *Magnifique*. It was not long, though, before the British captured her—admiring her structure and ornament so much, that they added to her carvings the crest of the Prince of Wales, and considered her peerless in all their fine navy.

During the last war with England she did service against her builders, and is still afloat, a fifty-gun ship of the Queen's, "an honor," says Mr. Brewster in his Rambles, "to Piscataqua shipwrights and to our coast oak."

www.ingramcontent.com/pod-product-compliance
Lightning Source LLC
Chambersburg PA
CBHW031815090426
42739CB00008B/1285